Praise for
Get Gen Z Into the Game

"*Get Gen Z Into the Game* is a game-changing leadership guide that merges practical wisdom with real-world application. Gen Z professionals are redefining the workplace, and Colleen McFarland provides the roadmap for leaders to navigate this shift successfully. More than just theory, McFarland lives what she teaches—mentorship, leadership development, and the power of people helping people. This book will transform how you lead, especially when combined with AI-driven insights for real-time change."

Peter Klein Founder, Educated Change

"*Get GenZ Into the Game* is the playbook for leaders committed to showing up for this remarkable generation as they navigate the workplace and beyond."

Jen Marr, Founder and CEO, Showing Up, LLC,
and author, *Showing Up* and *Lifting Up:
The Transformative Power of Supportive Leadership*

"Excellent advice for today's managers looking to get their Gen Z employees performing better."

Vijay Rangineni, Board Member,
Advisor and Strategic Investor, Dallas Venture Capital

"*Get Gen Z Into the Game* reveals a revolutionary approach to leadership—striking a balance between warmth and high expectations to guide Generation Z in the workplace. Colleen McFarland blends research and real-world insights to show how leaders can inspire connection, resilience, and productivity by adopting the Warm Demander style. This book is your blueprint to unlocking the potential of today's emerging workforce."

Dr. Merrylue Martin, Founder of the Job Joy Group, and author of *The Big Quit Survival Guide*

"I have seen first hand the transformative power of innovative technology in the insurance industry. It requires collaborative creative problem solving and engagement with multiple constituencies. *Get Gen Z Into the Game* is a book for any leader looking to ensure their future leaders develop the soft skills needed to compete in today's world."

Bill Suneson, Co-founder and CEO, Bindable

"As Gen Z's unique challenges and strengths reshape the workplace, Colleen McFarland masterfully blends insightful research with practical strategies to help leaders build authentic relationships and drive performance. This book is essential for leaders aiming to empower and connect with the youngest generation in the workforce through meaningful learning and impactful approaches."

David Barone, Head of Global Digital Learning at Takeda

"I agree with Colleen that leaders need to connect personally with their team members as well as push them to perform. When they do this, they provide early career employees a nurturing workplace home where they feel accepted and motivated to do their best and the result is better financial results for the organization."

Cheryl Murphy, CFO, Mercy Home for Boys and Girls

"*Get Gen Z into the Game* provides the playbook for how to address the unique challenges a generation raised with social media at their fingertips is bringing to the workplace. Colleen's five-step framework and Be-Social Method provide a practical path forward, making this an essential read for those invested in Gen Z's success. This book is invaluable. "

Kimberley Majury, Culture Builder and Global Marketer

"*Get Gen Z into the Game* provides managers a framework for coaching essential soft skills that young adults need to excel at work and in life. "

Renate Devin, Business Etiquette Professional, Speaker
and Founder of Boston School of Etiquette

"We can't expect the next generation to know what they haven't been taught. It's on us to guide, mentor, and create spaces where people thrive. With practical tools and deep insights, this book is a must read for anyone serious about sharing a strong, human-centered workplace."

Michelle Moffitt, psychotherapist, leadership coach,
and author of *Cracked Open: A Journey to a Resilient and
Independent Mindset*

"Colleen has it right when she says, 'Gen Zers need to feel their manager is genuinely interested in their success.' Becoming a warm demander leader will allow managers to demonstrate to Gen Zers they are not only genuinely interested in their success, but in them as people too. The end result will be a win-win for both parties as the Gen Zer gains trust in their manager and their manager develops a valuable relationship-based skillset in today's business world."

Dr. Ed Bray III, Senior Director of Human Resources, Ross Stores, Inc., and author of *Hello, Career*, an award-winning book about early career street smarts

GET
GEN
Z
INTO THE
GAME

The Playbook for Winning with Young Talent

COLLEEN MCFARLAND

Paulina Palms Publishing, Dunedin, Florida

The information provided within this book is for general entertainment and informational purposes only. This work depicts actual events, locales, and conversations as truthfully as possible, recalled from personal memories. In some examples throughout the book, names and certain identifying details have been changed to protect individuals' privacy

Author's note: In this book, when I discuss Gen Z, I am referring to observable trends and attitudes that have emerged as defining characteristics. I share these observations to provide insight into workplace behaviors that may resonate with many, but not all, members of Gen Z.

Although every effort has been made to ensure that information in this book was correct at press time, the author does not assume, and hereby disclaims, any liability to any party for any loss, damage, or disruption caused by errors or omissions, whether such errors or omissions result from negligence, accident, or any other cause.

Names: McFarland, Colleen, 1965- author.
Title: Get Gen Z into the game : the playbook for winning with young talent / Colleen McFarland.
Other titles: Get Generation Z into the game
Description: Dunedin, Florida : Paulina Palms Publishing, [2025]
Identifiers: LCCN: 2025903228 | ISBN: 9798992643008 (paperback) | 9798992643015 (Kindle) | 9798992643022 (ePub)
Subjects: LCSH: Communication in organizations. | Leadership. | Generation Z--Employment. | Employee motivation. | Social skills. | Teams in the workplace. | Corporate culture. | BISAC: BUSINESS & ECONOMICS / Workplace Culture. | BUSINESS & ECONOMICS / Mentoring & Coaching. | BUSINESS & ECONOMICS / Leadership.
Classification: LCC: HD30.3 .M34 2025 | DCC: 658.45--d23

Editorial services: Sandra Wendel, Write On, Inc.
Design: Yvonne Parks, PearCreative.ca

Contact the author at
Colleen@ColleenMcFarland.us
or 773-401-0897

For John, Daniel, and Chris

CONTENTS

FOREWORD

When I first started exploring the power of rejection, I discovered something profound—people fear failure less than what failure says about them. They fear looking unprepared, inexperienced, or not good enough.

And if there's one generation that's grappling with this fear more than ever, it's Gen Z.

Colleen McFarland's *Get Gen Z Into the Game* tackles one of the most pressing workplace challenges today: how do we help a generation raised on digital screens, social media, and instant feedback develop the real-world skills they need to succeed? How do we, as leaders, mentor them, challenge them, and push them to thrive in environments that demand resilience, adaptability, and confidence?

This book doesn't just talk about the problem—it offers a roadmap to transformation. Colleen introduces the Warm Demander leadership model, an approach that balances high expectations with personal connection. She unpacks how Gen

Z's struggle with loneliness and engagement isn't a character flaw—it's a symptom of a rapidly shifting world. And she lays out practical strategies to help leaders coach young employees into high-performing, confident contributors.

In my own journey, I've seen how embracing discomfort leads to greatness. The same principle applies to leadership. If you're managing Gen Z, working alongside them, or simply trying to understand them, this book will challenge you to step up—not just as a leader, but as a mentor who pushes young people toward their full potential.

Gen Z is ready to play. It's time to get them into the game.

Jia Jiang
Author of *Rejection Proof* and *The Art of Achieving Ambitious Things*
Keynote Speaker, Entrepreneur

INTRODUCTION

When my son Daniel was a freshman at Georgetown, I came to visit him for their family weekend events. I was excited to meet his friends and their parents. Daniel quickly told me his friends were busy with their parents. When I suggested we attend some of the planned events, he told me he wasn't interested in attending any of them. His only suggestion for the weekend was for us to go to Starbucks where he could study, and I could drink my tea.

After some more discussion, we agreed we'd go to two of the planned events. He'd pick one and I'd pick one. He picked the tailgate before the soccer game that he did not want to go to. I picked a lecture in the business school titled "Are you a Creator or Borrower? The Surprising Habit of the Most Successful Young People."

Daniel and I went to the lecture. The lecturer, Eric Koester, took the stage. He walked across the stage waving his hands as he spoke. He had a friendly Midwestern style. I liked him immediately.

He was an entrepreneur, and he'd been teaching entrepreneurship at Georgetown for a few years. He told us that one year prior, he wanted to quit teaching. He had looked up what his former students were doing after graduating and hardly any were entrepreneurs, so he decided that he had failed and wanted out.

He let Georgetown know he was done teaching because he wasn't any good at it. Georgetown told him that he had to teach one more semester since, after all, it was August. He then had a conversation with a friend who was also an entrepreneur. He vented his frustration about this situation.

His friend said, "Why don't you just mix it up? Totally change the course because it doesn't matter, you are only teaching it one more time."

As Eric told the story, I pictured them drinking beer while they were talking and brainstorming how he could change the course. After conversing for a bit, they decided Eric should have his students write books. Both Eric and his friend had written a book when they were in their twenties, and it had resulted in them meeting people they never would have met before. They recognized that the process of writing a book, for each of them, had changed the direction of their lives.

Later that August, during the first day of the entrepreneurship class, Eric showed up with his new syllabus. He displayed it and let his students know that most of their grade that semester would be based on a 20,000-word manuscript for a nonfiction book on any topic they were interested in.

The students were dumbfounded. This is not the class they signed up for.

Eric told them this project would give them license to reach out and meet people doing things they want to do or are interested in exploring. About twenty-two of the twenty-four students finished a manuscript by the end of the semester.

Eric then showed the manuscripts to a friend of his in the publishing world. He didn't tell him where the manuscripts came from. His friend said, "These are really pretty good!"

Then Eric told him his students wrote the manuscripts. His publisher friend encouraged Eric to stick around Georgetown for another semester and work with the students on the editing process. He also said that if Eric helped the students edit, he would publish the books.

So Eric decided to teach another semester. And, of course, the result was twenty-two newly published authors.

As Eric finished his story, he invited a dozen or so of those students to walk across the stage holding up their books. He read the titles. One book was about video games, one book was about millennials and finance, another book on soccer recruiting in India, another about beer.

I was blown away.

My son and I left the lecture and headed to the tailgate for the soccer game that we were not going to go to. After we got our food and grabbed a seat, I told Daniel how much I liked the lecture and asked him what he thought. He said it was interesting. I mentioned that I thought the professor had to be from the Midwest. Daniel instantly looked him up on his smartphone and smiled at me. "Mom, it says he went to Marquette."

"Very funny," I said, sensing a setup. Daniel knows I love Marquette University, where I went to college. He has several times in the past teased me saying someone I am admiring "went to Marquette," at which I'd excitedly reply, "Really? That's awesome!" at which he would joke, "Just kidding."

This time was different. Daniel said, "No, he really did go to Marquette." To which I replied, "Fantastic. I'm going to send him a note right now."

I sent Eric a message through LinkedIn and eventually got on the phone with him. We talked about Marquette and about Georgetown, his course, and my son Daniel.

Then I told Eric how much I enjoyed his lecture and how I love that he was teaching young adults how to network.

I told him that his book-writing process was amazing and I thought it would work for anyone. I encouraged him to offer the technique to people outside of academia. I suggested he could help so many people get better at networking.

He told me he didn't think it would work for older people because we are not open to the process of exploring and learning. He said an older person would come to the class with a book already written in their mind. I respectfully disagreed and said that I thought lots of working professionals would benefit from this book-writing process and be open to where the journey took them. I also offered to help him in any way I could because I think he's amazing!

I also shared with him that I'm a management consultant who helps executives lead their people through workplace change. And that my passion is business networking.

I think everyone should embrace networking practices because, when you do, you are not only better at work, you are also more confident and happier.

I told him about the workshops I run for a not-for-profit in Chicago called the Career Transition Center. It's where I teach my networking methodology that I call the Be-Social Method.

We finished the call and agreed to stay in touch.

Eric ended up piloting this book-writing process with a group of working professionals in Washington, DC. He told me the results were really positive. He then asked me to help him with scaling his book-writing process beyond Georgetown to people outside of academia. I happily agreed.

Part of the help I provided Eric was to try out his book-writing process along with others in our cohort of working professionals. This included "an author-chat" with Eric—a fifteen-minute time slot. During my own one-on-one with Eric, he asked me, "What do you want to research and write about?"

I replied, "Business networking."

To which, he sighed and said, "You already know about business networking. Isn't there anything else you are curious about? This is a great opportunity to learn something new."

I smiled at the question. I had just demonstrated what Eric predicted older authors would do: show up with a book that I already had written in my mind.

After a brief pause, I said, "Yes, I want to know why some young adults have started coming to my business networking workshops. Usually, my participants are people in their forties, fifties, or sixties, and occasionally someone in their late thirties. But recently, I've been having a few people in their early twenties show up. I don't get it. Why are they worried about business networking at such a young age? Why aren't they deciding which happy hour to go to?"

Eric said, "Good! Go find that out."

GEN Z IS LONELY

Following Eric's process, I did the research and learned the following:

- Members of Generation Z born 1997 to 2012 who are now showing up in the workplace are struggling with loneliness and it's making them sick. In 2017, generational expert Jean Twenge described Gen Z as being on the brink of the worst mental health crisis in decades.

- People who struggle with loneliness also struggle at work. Lonely team members are less engaged, less innovative, more likely to miss work, more likely to go on short-term disability, and quit.

- These problems are causing them to perform poorly at work and hitting their organization's bottom line due to higher healthcare costs, increased absenteeism, lower productivity, and higher turnover.

TOO MANY IN GEN Z
(born 1997 - 2012)

1. ARE LONELY & FEEL UNSAFE

2. HAVE MENTAL HEALTH ISSUES

3. AVOID IN REAL LIFE PARTS OF JOB

4. HAVE HIGHER TURNOVER

WORK PLACE SOLUTIONS

1. PROVIDE THEM THEIR DATA

2. EQUIP YOUR MANAGERS

3. IMPROVE ONLINE EXPERIENCE

4. LEVERAGE PEOPLE DATA

I learned that Gen Z is lonely and it's making them sick.

GEN Z LONELINESS IMPACTS YOUR BOTTOMLINE

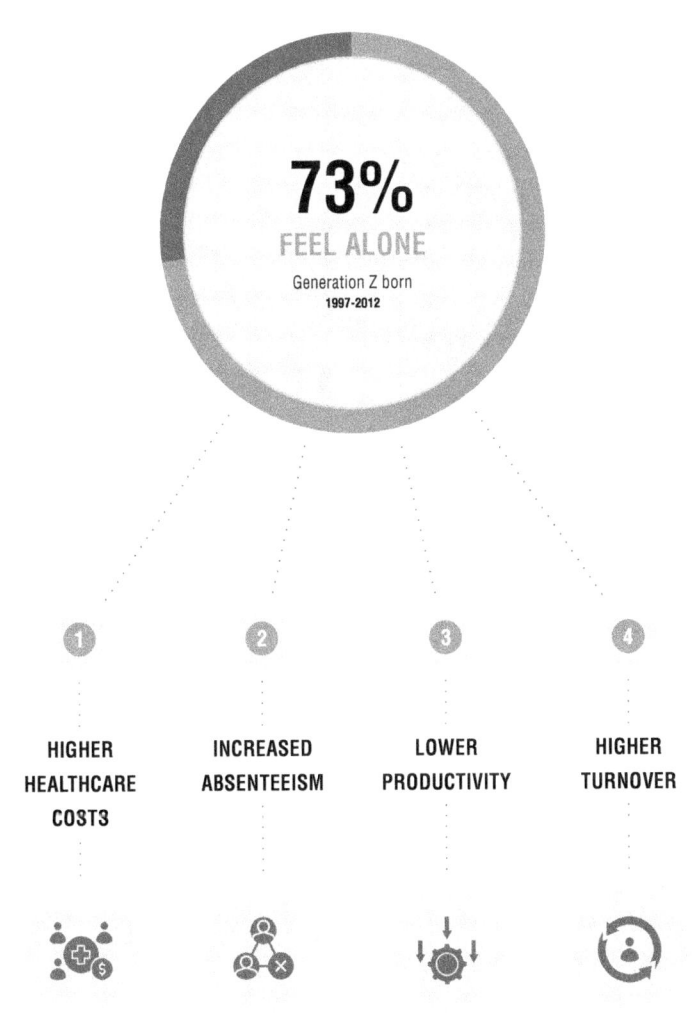

73%

FEEL ALONE

Generation Z born
1997-2012

1	**2**	**3**	**4**
HIGHER HEALTHCARE COST3	INCREASED ABSENTEEISM	LOWER PRODUCTIVITY	HIGHER TURNOVER

This realization broke my heart, and I wanted to know what I could do about it. I thought there must be something that could be done in the workplace. I continued my research on this topic including dozens of interviews with experts.

My book published in 2020 is based on the tech challenges for all of us, but especially for Gen Z.

In April 2020, I published the book titled *Disconnected*. My book digs into how technology has not only changed how we work, but changed us, too, especially Gen Z. It's made us less authentically connected with others. As a result, many people, especially young adults, are lonely. I offer four workplace solutions in *Disconnected*—one of which is to equip the manager to better lead young adults who are data driven and tech savvy and yet struggle with making in real life (IRL) connections.

After I published *Disconnected*, my readers wanted to know more about what managers specifically could do. Plus, just about everyone I talked to about *Disconnected* and Gen Z told me about a preteen, teen, or young adult they knew personally who was struggling with mental health.

It seemed to me that so many people were seeing just a sliver of what's going on with Gen Z, but hardly anyone was talking about it as something larger that needed to be addressed.

My friend Jim shared with me his frustrations with the early career employees at his company, where he is the president. They are not producing, and it seems to Jim like several of them are not able to handle the normal stress of work. He genuinely doesn't know what to do about the problem.

He and others inspired me to do the research that resulted in this book.

I have learned that many workplace leaders like Jim are not aware that their younger colleagues are struggling with loneliness per se. However, they are seeing that this cohort is different from those who came before them, and managers are finding it confounding.

I started seeing article after article with this same sentiment. For example, one report in 2023 ResumeBuilder.com surveyed 1,344 managers and business leaders and found the following:

- 74% believe Gen Z is more difficult to work with than other generations.

- 12% have fired a Gen Zer less than one week after their start date.

- Being too easily offended is a top reason Gen Zers get fired.

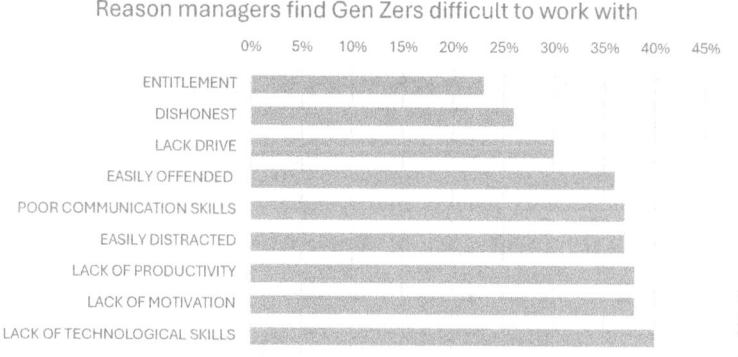

Reason managers find Gen Zers difficult to work with

EYES ROLLING

To me it feels like some of these leaders are rolling their eyes and complaining about their younger employees and colleagues. The complaints sound like this:

- They're invisible. They prefer to stay at their desk rather than join others in the conference room.

- They're dull. They can't really make small talk.

- They're wallflowers. At our work events, they don't mingle.

- They suffer in silence. They seem afraid to ask anyone for help.

WHY THE BAD REPUTATION?

Gen Z has been challenging to work with for various reasons. They often bring little work experience following college graduation. Many had parents who encouraged them to focus on academics while forgoing even part-time jobs. Plus, they have grown up on screens, so they frequently bring lower levels of emotional intelligence than previous generations.

Too many young adults are struggling with loneliness and related mental health issues. These problems are causing them to perform poorly at work and hitting the organization's bottom line due to higher healthcare costs, increased absenteeism, lower productivity, and higher turnover.

I reached out and connected with experts on suicide and supportive care to learn more. Through them, I learned about a term that educators use called *warm demander*.

WARM DEMANDER

Warm demander is used to describe a teaching style. It was coined by Judith Kleinfeld in her 1975 research on effective teachers in Alaskan schools.

Kleinfeld described teachers who provide personal warmth with high expectations as warm demanders. These teachers insist on high performance while providing a supportive and structured environment. Since Kleinfeld's research, several other studies have been done since to document the success warm demander teachers had with specific populations of students.

As I was reading through the studies, I was struck by how Gen Z workers struggle with many of the same things the students in the studies struggled with, including:

- Motivation,
- Feeling valued,
- Cultural challenges, and
- Adapting to new environments and new expectations.

THE BEST LEADERS OF CHANGE ARE WARM DEMANDERS

Additionally, I see how the warm demander teacher antidote parallels successes I had in my decades of working with leaders who drive massive changes in their organizations such as integrating acquired companies and putting in new technology or new processes that require team members to learn radically new ways of working.

These leaders have stakeholders who struggle with the similar challenges when facing change, such as wondering after the workplace change is implemented whether they will still be valued or if they would be able to perform their job well enough to keep it.

What I do is coach the leaders on how to build relationships with those they are leading and to be as clear as possible on the work they need to do to get the change in place, including what success looks like.

Like the warm demander teachers, the best leaders of change measure progress and celebrate accomplishments.

You can say (and I do say this now), I want these workplace leaders of change to be warm demander leaders.

I have seen time and time again when these leaders are able to bring the right mix of warm and demanding, their teams make progress faster, handle the stress of the change better, and rightly feel proud of their accomplishments. It's awesome.

WHAT GEN Z WANTS

I found myself nodding as I read a *Wall Street Journal* report that said Gen Z workers struggle to feel connections with their colleagues and may need some additional guidance on workplace norms, particularly through mentors. The same report called out that "Gen Z wants security and this chance to matter."

I networked with a friend's daughter who was twenty-four years old and looking for a new job. She told me she was looking for a company with good retirement benefits. She wanted a place she could stay for her whole career. When she said this to me, it struck me how different this was from millennials who are known for having two, three, or four jobs within ten years.

Rohin Shani, author of *The Z Factor; How to Lead Gen Z to Workplace Success*, told me Gen Z employees want to find a secure future-proof place to work. They want to work with smart leaders that they can trust.

Shani also told me Gen Z wants to know their company's biggest problems. They want to work on them and will even do so on their own time.

Tim Elmore, author of *A New Kind of Diversity: Making the Different Generations on Your Team a Competitive Advantage* and CEO of the Atlanta-based Growing Leaders organization, adds this key point to the conversation: "The age of authority is dropping. Consider this: young professionals often enter their careers with a greater insight into social media and how to monetize it. They seem to understand what young consumers want, and they possess deeper intuition on where culture is going. At the same time, the age of maturity is rising. Several university deans have told me, '26 is the new 18.' They are maturing socially and emotionally later than previous generations of young graduates."

Because of this combination, not just any manager will do. Managers needed are those that excel in modeling and coaching relationship-building skills in addition to driving bottom-line results.

Gen Z influencer Christian Hodges explains that Gen Z employees need mentorship to foster personal accountability, professional growth, and spiritual guidance. He explains Gen Z should not be left on their own to find all three. He calls on leaders to answer the call to mentor and do so in a genuine way.

He suggests each leader find a young person who reminds them of themselves, who they can be real with, for example, be "willing to divulge [their own] highs and lows." In this way, they establish trust and are better able to counsel Gen Z where they are.

I love this. It sounds like a warm demander mentor. Like Hodges, I recommend you do this in your personal life for at least one young adult you know. If not for a colleague, consider a nephew, niece, or neighbor. It's a great place to start. We need to help these amazing young adults who are our future leaders.

At work, I want you to be a warm demander for each member of your team. I have written this book for you and all workplace leaders. I want you to become a warm demander leader especially for Gen Z team members.

My hope is that eye rolling stops and, instead, awesome leaders, like you, roll up your sleeves and connect with these young adults who need you and, by the way, are amazing at so many tasks that leverage their tech-savvy, data driven, and continuous learner attributes.

THE BE-SOCIAL METHOD

You are well positioned to help those you lead transform from feeling lonely to feeling secure. You can show them how to become part of a network of people that supports, encourages, and inspires each other.

This works because you are older. You developed your social skills a long time ago when you were young and before there was an internet.

- As a result, you know *how to meet people* in real life.

- You also know how to establish rapport with colleagues and *get to know* them.

- You have the ability to *bring people together* that you know to solve problems, or just to have some fun!

- And you—yes, you—know *how to ask others for help* when you need it.

You may be a bit rusty with some of the practices related to developing relationships. You may even find some of the practices related to maintaining relationships hard. However, I know you have seen all of these practices done, over and over again in your lifetime. You know how to build and maintain relationships.

Therefore, you are an excellent candidate to master my networking methodology, the Be-Social Method, and warmly demand those you lead to do the same—and when you do, you will rightly feel proud of your accomplishment. Plus, I know this and I bet you do, too, that it's fun to push others to grow and see them win.

Frankly, isn't it our obligation to do whatever we can to develop those who follow us?

You can be a leader that strikes a balance with those you lead. You can provide personal warmth with high expectations. You can connect authentically with those you lead and push them to excel. You can let them know you want them to "Go for it!" You can push them to do the work to change from feeling lonely to feeling secure.

You can be the leader who forms genuine relationships with them and pushes them to engage at work with others, to excel and to win.

THREE STEPS FOR YOU

1. Hone your leadership skills to become a warm demander leader. Determine if you need to work on being more warm or more demanding or both.

2. Master my networking methodology, the Be-Social Method, which I explain in detail in this book. It will give you the vocabulary to use when coaching your team members on the practices they need to master in order for them to perform better at work and to be happier.

3. Model and coach the Be-Social Method practices. Demonstrate these practices to your team in an obvious way. Coach each of your team members on the Be-Social practices they need to work on.

When you do this, you will see your team members transform to visible, dynamic, collaborative, and secure go-getters who win and are happier.

HOW TO READ THIS BOOK

There is a lot to know about being a warm demander leader. Treat the table of contents of this book like a drop-down menu. Scan for what you want to learn more about and go directly there.

Identify what you want out of this book. Having a clear outcome is a powerful yet often overlooked tactic when reading a nonfiction book. This book has stories that illustrate how the warm demander leadership style combined with the Be-Social Method is transformative, both in terms of having more productive employees and in seeing employees transform into happier, healthier humans.

Consider a few questions you want the book to answer for you. Then go look for the answers.

Use the structure of the book as a guide. The book is made up of three parts. The structure is put in place to help you better understand the book's contents. Do not let the structure limit you. Jump into any chapter that interests you.

Part I makes the case for the warm demander (W-D) leader and provides you the W-D Lens to use to assess your leadership style. It provides illustrations of the leader types that are not quite warm enough or demanding enough to be considered a warm demander.

Part II walks through the Be-Social Method and its building blocks including the networking practices.

Part III introduces you to the Five-Step Approach to use for analyzing and coaching your team members on the key soft skills they need for workplace relationship building. It illustrates its use with four examples.

Knowledge is not power. Knowledge is only potential power. Nothing will happen unless you take action. Reflect on what you as a leader can do to address the loneliness of our young adults both at work and in your personal life. Consider how you can be the person in your organization who drives the development of young adults, and, as a result, you will provide growth and success for your company.

PART I

Gen Z team members in the workplace need warm demander leaders to get their performance to improve. Specifically, they need leaders who will push them to develop their key soft skills and build their network of support so they can jump in and work together on your organization's toughest challenges.

These young adults in the workplace are learn-it-alls, and they are earnest, data driven, and cautious. They love training and respond to authentic leaders' direction to develop new skills.

While not all leaders are warm demanders, any leader can transform to be a warm demander. To do so, they need to work on being either more warm or more demanding or both. When they do this work, they will—

- Be more effective at getting early career employees to perform,

- Find that their team members who have been holding back will engage, and

- Become the leader that team members love working for.

A warm demander's team members will happily go above and beyond for them, and as a result their team will grow and win. This part helps you assess your own leadership style on your journey to becoming a warm demander.

ONE

WARMLY DEMANDING RELATIONSHIP BUILDING PRACTICES

David S., a tech executive, told me this story:

BUSINESS-MINDED PRIEST

One of my mentors growing up was our local priest. His dad was a successful businessman. I lived in a rural community. His dad had a law firm. He had a fleet of private jets that he chartered. He had a company that fueled all the jets at the Toledo airport. He had all kinds of businesses that were highly successful.

His son, our priest, grew up in this business world. He was on the board of all his dad's companies. He was a business-minded priest. He knew that I was different than others in our small town in that I wanted to get out of Dodge. He kind of took me under his wing from junior high through high school. He taught me what it takes to be successful in business.

In the town I grew up in, there was a little bit of twang in the way people speak. I spent a lot of time with him, and he would always correct the way I spoke. He would say, "If you're going to go into business, you've got to learn how to speak well. I'm going to correct you so that you can learn the right way to speak." And so he did.

He took me to spend time with his dad and brothers who ran those companies. I received a lot of learning experiences with those guys and during dinners.

My parents were teaching me manners, but there was a completely different level of having dinner when you're at the country club, whch I had never experienced before. For my family, Ponderosa, the steak house, was high end. So going through those experiences with him taught me a lot. He was critical of me in a way to prepare me for what I was about to do or what I wanted to do.

MENTORS OF SOCIAL PRACTICES

David had a mentor in his life who insisted he work on the social practices he needed to be successful in the business world that he would eventually enter.

Leaders in the workplace now, like David, were given ample opportunity in their adolescence to develop social skills and related soft skills. They had parents and teachers who insisted they engage in conversations at home, at school, and in their community. This expectation continued when they left home, attended college or trade schools, or entered the world of work. These experiences were all in person. As a result, their soft skills were well honed by the time they were twenty-one and in the workplace.

Today, leaders are reporting seeing their early career employees being slower to get up the learning curve at work. They are struggling in the soft skills portion of their job.

Early career employees are slower to pick up on nuanced informal rules or practices (these run the gamut from making eye contact when talking to someone to being pleasantly persistent in following up with a team member who agreed to complete a task) that other early career employees before them absorbed and adopted, without anyone intervening to explain. They need leaders to encourage this professional growth, build in accountability for it, and monitor it.

Plus, employees who work virtually or hybrid are not making many, if any, friends at work. They are not establishing and building relationships at work the way they need to be. They are missing those work friends who help them get things done faster by showing them the ropes—or just helping them cope with some of the BS of work by sharing a laugh or venting. Get these employees in the office. There they can see the value of workplace relationships, and with your help figure out how to build them.

PSYCHOLOGICALLY FRAGILE

Experts who pay attention to mental health trends believe that Gen Z workers are psychologically fragile. Why? Some say it's because they did not have enough free play when they were kids. Others say it's because they spend too much time in the virtual world on their smartphones, away from their time in the real world where these skills are learned. Others say that the months of mandated remote learning during the pandemic is the main culprit.

In his book *Free to Learn*, Peter Gray explains that young adults who didn't get enough unsupervised play time as children missed out on learning how to push the limits, deal with fear, solve problems, deal with anger, and get along with peers. In the workplace, these early career employees are not equipped for the stresses of work life.

However, Gen Z has demonstrated that when given clear direction and proper incentive, they will follow a manager's instructions. That means leaders of this cohort can design assignments into their employee's job that develop specific weak soft skills.

When an early career employee is told an assignment is part of their job and will be part of their performance evaluation, they will do it. This is especially true if the assignment will be measured, and they trust their leader.

When a leader requires their team members to do assignments related to the Be-Social practices I will describe later in this book, the employee will develop the key soft skills they need for doing awesome work with their coworkers and customers.

When leaders take this approach, they will see their team members' performance improve and their confidence grow.

CHANGE MANAGEMENT

When I started hearing that today's early career employees are struggling with the adjustment to the workplace, my research led me to learn that the youngest members of the workforce are the loneliest.

Around this time, I connected with James Mazza, an expert on teen suicide and the co-creator of DBT Steps—a school-based social and emotional learning program for adolescents. He helped me understand the role that teachers and other leaders can play in pushing students to develop the skills they need to cope with the normal ups and downs of life and the importance of tracking progress.

Because of that conversation, I attended the 2022 NYS Suicide Prevention Conference: Fostering Connection Across the Lifespan, where I heard Dr. Mazza and others speak about the progress their DBT Steps program had made in Central New York and Brooklyn. In addition to Dr. Mazza, I heard principal Alexandra Hernandez speak about how she transformed her Brooklyn high school to one of a faculty and staff of warm demanders.

I had never heard the warm demander term before. A quick Google search revealed to me that is a term used by educators that applies to teachers and others in the school setting that interact with students in such a way that they inspire them to engage and achieve.

I loved this term and started using it in my change management practice. It encapsulates what my decades of working with leaders who drive change has shown me.

- Warm: Leaders who get changes implemented well are adept at building genuine relationships with the people they are partnering with and leading.

- Demander: They are also proficient at communicating their expectations and getting progress against those expectations measured and communicated frequently.

These leaders who successfully drive change in the workplace are, then, warm demander leaders.

When employees need to change their mindset and behaviors in order to be all in for a dramatic workplace change like a digital transformation, the introduction of AI, or a merger of companies, they often resist. Because, let's face it, who wants to do the extra work that a dramatic workplace change brings? But when the person charged with leading the transformation adopts a warm demander leadership style, their people are less resistant to do the extra work. They trust their leader.

Warm demander leaders are able to connect authentically with their team members. They genuinely want to know their team members personally and share parts of their personal life with them. Plus, they push their team to win, and winning feels good.

They insist everyone not only engages but stretches themselves. The result is lots of wins and growth for team members. When a team member is pushed to grow by taking on work that they have never done before, they can find it scary. However, when they trust the leader who says, "You can do this," they will do it. I have seen this happen, time and time again, in the workplace. Researchers have been showing for decades that this happens in schools.

WARM DEMANDERS FOR YOUR EARLY CAREER EMPLOYEES

Warm demanders are the right leaders to manage today's early career employees. Today's early career employees are cautious with everyone including their direct boss. They will hold back. However, like employees being pushed to embrace dramatic change in the workplace, once they sense a leader genuinely cares about them, they will be all in and ready to grow as needed into their role.

Leaders, I urge you to set your team members up to win. Adopt the style of a leader who is good at driving change in your organizations. Be a warm demander leader. Become awesome at warmly demanding your team members do the work needed to strengthen their soft skills so that they can become top performers.

TWO

HOW TO TELL IF YOU ARE A WARM DEMANDER

When I first meet a leader, I am able to quickly assess what skills they need to work on in order to become the warm demander leader they need to be. To help you assess your own skills, I have developed the W-D (Warm Demander) Lens.

The W-D Lens will show if you are ready to inspire your early career employees to work on their essential soft skills. If you are not a warm demander yet, the W-D Lens will show you what you need to work on to become a warm demander.

W-D LENS

There are four quadrants in the W-D Lens—one for each of the leadership types.

Expert: The lower left quadrant represents the expert type. The expert demonstrates weak relationship building skills with their team members. This gives them a low warmth score. They also demonstrate being weak at setting performance expectations with their team members, and are not well prepared to provide their team members feedback on their performance. This gives them a low demander score.

Buddy: The lower right quadrant represents the buddy type. The buddy demonstrates strong relationship building skills with their team members. This gives them a high warmth score. They are, however, weak at setting performance expectations with their team members and not well equipped to provide their team members feedback on their performance. This gives them a low demander score.

Driver: The upper left quadrant represents the driver type. The driver demonstrates weak relationship building skills with their team members. This gives them a low warmth score. They demonstrate being strong at setting performance expectations with their team members and providing their team members feedback on their performance. This gives them a high demander score.

Warm demander: The upper right quadrant represents the warm demander type. The warm demander demonstrates strong relationship building skills with their team members. This gives them a high warmth score. They demonstrate being strong at setting performance expectations with their team members and providing their team members feedback on their performance. This gives them a high demander score. This is your goal.

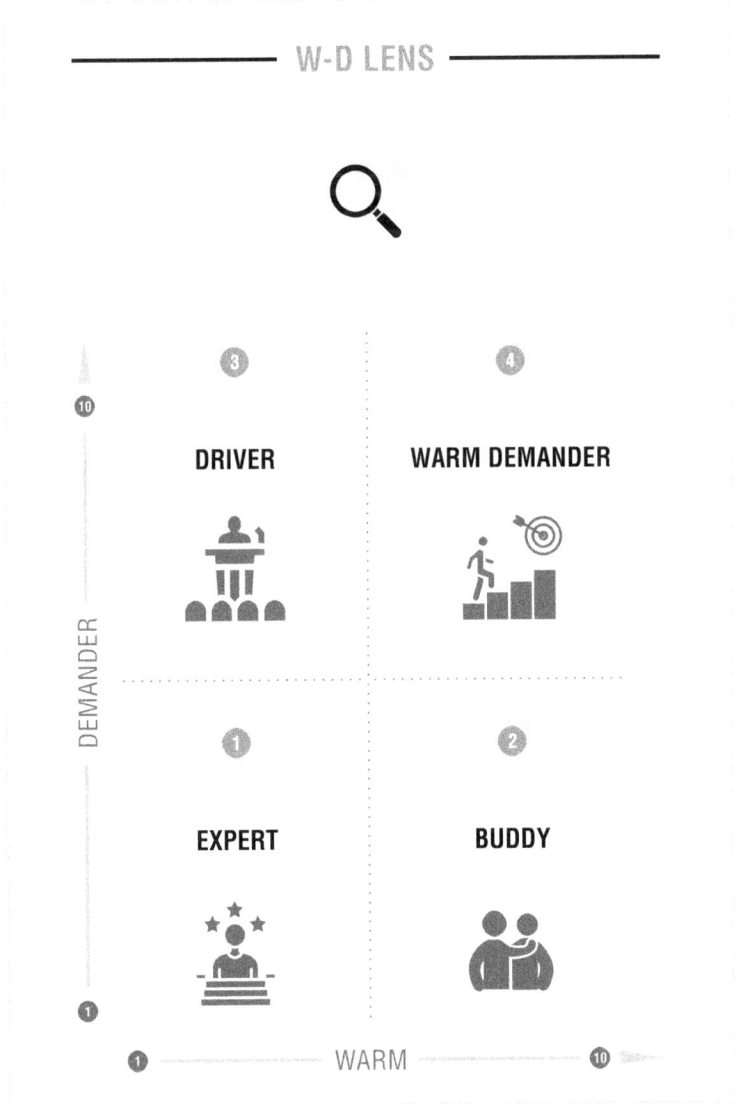

ASSESS YOURSELF

1. Familiarize yourself with the four W-D types by reading chapters 3 through 6 in this book.

2. Then answer the questions in the table here, to assist you in determining which W-D type you see yourself as (expert, buddy, driver, warm demander).

3. Score 1 point for each yes answer. Sum the points for each column (expert, buddy, driver, warm demander).

4. The column with the highest score is your dominant W-D type.

Assess Your W-D Type
Add the points of each column to see your dominant W-D Type

Expert	Buddy	Driver	Warm Demander
Do you rely more on your technical skills than on interpersonal skills? Yes=1 No=0	Do you often prioritize personal relationships over work-related tasks? Yes=1 No=0	Do you set high expectations and expect your team to meet them without much guidance? Yes=1 No=0	Do you balance giving clear instructions with listening to your team's input? Yes=1 No=0
Do you avoid asking your team members for feedback on your management style? Yes=1 No=0	Do you find it challenging to set clear expectations for your team? Yes=1 No=0	Do you often use a direct and assertive communication style? Yes=1 No=0	Do you encourage your team to take ownership of their work while offering support? Yes=1 No=0

Are you hesitant to form close relationships with your team members?	Do you frequently check in with your team members about their personal lives?	Do you prioritize results over relationships?	Are you able to provide constructive feedback in a way that motivates your team?
Yes=1 No=0	Yes=1 No=0	Yes=1 No=0	Yes=1 No=0
Do you struggle to delegate tasks effectively?	Do you avoid giving constructive feedback to avoid hurting feelings?	Do you rarely offer praise or recognition for your team's efforts?	Do you build strong relationships with your team members while maintaining high expectations?
Yes=1 No=0	Yes=1 No=0	Yes=1 No=0	Yes=1 No=0
Column total:	Column total:	Column total:	Column total:

1. Show the W-D Lens to your manager or a trusted professional friend who has worked with you. Explain the four types and ask them which type they see you as.

2. Show the W-D Lens to two of your past team members. Explain the four types and ask them which type they see you as.

3. Compare your assessment to others you have asked to weigh in and then summarize the result.

Your W-D Assessment					
Your Assessment	Your Manager's Assessment	Trusted Professional Friend	Past Team Member #1	Past Team Member #2	Summary
Expert	Buddy	Buddy	Buddy	Expert	**Buddy**

An example of how to assess what type of leader you are and what others think you are, using the W-D Lens

After your assessment, consider if your style is working for you. Is your team performing as needed? If so, great! If your team is not performing, explore the possibility that the team needs a warm demander leader.

If you are not a warm demander leader, decide if you are open to working on being one. If not, look for a job that is a better fit for your leadership style. If you are willing to work on being a warm demander leader, hooray! The world needs more warm demanders. Thanks for being open to doing the work you need to do.

HOW A WARM DEMANDER RESPONDS

"I handpicked you, unless you think I'm an idiot, you belong here. I'm going to show you what you need to know. Listen to me. Converse with me. Let's interact. Let's exchange ideas and you'll see just how good you can be," Terry C., a VP for a multinational mass media and entertainment company, said to Manny.

When Manny started in the professional world, he suffered from impostor syndrome, questioning if he really belonged in his position at his company. Manny explained to me that the odds are stacked against you when you grow up in an urban Hispanic ghetto, like he did, in New Jersey. It's hard to shake some insecurities even when you've had success.

Terry, who took Manny under his wing, was a tough veteran of their industry plus very intelligent. Terry would push back when Manny questioned if he rightfully belonged on his team.

Manny started off at the local division of the multinational company, which is at the local media stations. Terry had heard that Manny was a young seller with no experience but a diamond in the rough. Terry made an effort to get to know Manny by interacting with him at company events.

Through those conversations, Terry shared with Manny that even though he was an Irish kid from the south side of Chicago, he was a tremendous Yankee fan, like Manny. They hit it off right away.

Also, it turned out, Terry was an incredible Notre Dame fan, which was where Manny went to college. They started hanging out at company events. When the spot came open on Terry's team, he said, "I want you to come up with me. I think you'll do great. It's a national level role, you will have much more responsibility and much more exposure to others in the organization."

He showed Manny the ropes, preparing him to eventually take over the department.

HOW A WARM DEMANDER RELATES

When La'Mone started in her new role in the food manufacturing business, her boss, Charles S., said, "Hey, just so you know, you are not my first choice. And it's nothing personal against you. It's just you don't have the experience I'm looking for. But with you and I working together, you'll get that experience. You've got a year to get up to speed. Here's some things that you're going to need to know in order to be successful in your role."

Charles was the regional HR business partner for the food manufacturing business.

When La'Mone started, Charles was up front with her. Charles let her know she was not qualified for her role. La'Mone didn't have the experience or a degree that would have qualified her.

When the role opened up, Charles was told by his vice president to hire her. She was not his choice for the role. Yet he was committed to developing her and doing everything he could to make her successful

Charles told La'Mone a story about one of the toughest lessons he ever learned.

"When I first got out of the army, in my very first job, I got laid off. I remember it was midnight when they laid me off. I'm sitting in the parking lot thinking through this. I didn't have a college degree and I thought, man, what am I going to do now? I didn't have a job. I didn't have a livelihood, and I have all these bills that I had to pay. I made the decision that very night to go enroll in college. I told myself I will never be in a position again where I don't have options."

After sharing the story, Charles said to La'Mone, "Look, if this company goes bankrupt tomorrow, what are you going to do? You've got nothing to fall back on. And not to mention, they can treat you however they want to treat you because they know you don't have options."

As a result of this conversation, La'Mone enrolled in college. As of my interview with Charles, she was about a year away from graduating with her degree in human resources.

Charles doesn't work with La'Mone currently, but he still hears from her. Charles reflects, "So, it's kind of cool to see her evolution. See how she's transforming into someone who has options rather than someone who could be held in the one place because she doesn't have a choice."

Leaders, use the W-D Lens to assess yourself, as you get familiar with the four W-D types described in the following four chapters.

If you concluded you are a warm demander leader, go lead the teams that are most critical to your company's success and future. Most likely your team will be composed of a fair number of Gen Z teams since they are 30 percent of the workforce and will continue to grow. Your warm demander style will resonate with this cohort.

If you conclude you are not a warm demander and you have a team that is not performing as well as it could, do the work to become a warm demander. Start with assessing if you want to be warmer or more demanding or both.

THREE

THE EXPERT

The Sharp-Tongued Manager

Kimberly R., a visual merchandiser, told me this story:

Scott was responsible for setting up a new design center for our company and was building his team. I became one of the five people on this team. I was the only woman and the only person to join this team from outside of the company. Scott had recruited me.

Scott was cold, but he was really pretty awesome. He helped me.

I was super gung-ho about my job at the time. I was super type A, really wanting to do the best job to forward my trajectory. I was like a career person. I would get in at seven a.m. and get to work. While waiting for Scott to get in, I would email with my questions.

He was a very leisurely boss. He would stroll in with his Starbucks around 9:30. He was slow to wake up and get started. He'd go into his office and close the door. So I would be waiting to go in and chat with him about what I had already emailed him, about what I'd gotten done.

I remember distinctly one time knocking on his door. When he said, "Come in," I went in. I then said, "Scott, I've got so many things to talk to you about."

He asked, "How many?"

I said, "Let me see." I counted up my items and I said, "Ten."

He responded, "Narrow that down to two, and then come back and talk to me."

It was great direction that has stuck with me. It helped me to problem-solve on my own, so I could move forward. I would have a problem and then say to myself, "I'm not going to go to him with that. I can figure that out! Yes, I can figure that out." And I did.

I'm so glad that I worked for him. He helped me grow. That job gave me the building blocks of my visual merchandising career.

The Player Coach

David S., the tech exec, told me about Paul. In his words, Paul was a really bright engineer and he was a player coach in the lab. He was a manager and had a bunch of engineers working for him. He was as much an engineer as he was a manager. All the engineers loved him, and it worked.

Paul was so good at failure analysis. One time the fire department thought our product caused a house fire. We sent Paul out to troubleshoot with the fire department. He actually found the defects in the wiring of the house, not in our product.

Paul reported to the director of engineering, who reported to me. The director took another position, and that director position was open. Paul came to me and said, "I want the job."

I said, "Paul you can't do that job."

He said, "I think I can, and I'd like a chance to do it."

I said "Paul, here's your problem. You are a detailed engineer. In the lab that works. You need to understand the details. You do failure analysis and work with your team. As a director you can't do that. You will have multiple teams."

He said, "I really want this job. It's the next level of my career."

I said, "I'm going to tell you right now I think you're going to fail. I want to get that on the table. But I am going to give you the chance. We're going to have an agreement going in. You're going to take the job. After a month or two, we're both going to sit down and be honest with each other. I'm going to be honest with you about your performance. And you're going to be honest with me about whether or not you actually like doing the job. Then if I think you're failing or you think the job is not for you, you get your old job back. No harm. No foul."

So two months later, we have our meeting. And I said, "Paul what do you think?"

He said, "I think I'm failing, and I want my old job back."

I gave him his old job back. He never looked to do anything beyond that job, because that was what he was good at, and he loved it.

THE EXPERT

The expert is a leader who has not only mastered their function but is exemplary at it. They are confident and capable.

If they lead a design team like Kimberly's boss, Scott, they can please a customer by addressing their design needs flawlessly. If they lead an engineering team like Paul, they solve the hard problems that stump others.

Experts are admired for their proficiency at their craft. They are head and shoulders above the rest.

Experts, however, do not radiate warmth or expect their team members to grow. It's not something they value. They may not even talk with team members beyond the essential assignment of work and checking on status. They rarely socialize with team members and rarely express pleasure or displeasure with performance. They lead by example.

Team members who perform well for them are those who admire their expertise and hope to someday become as expert as they are.

Many of today's early career employees will not be all in for an expert leader. When they do not feel the manager is genuinely interested in their success and do not feel pushed to develop skills needed, they won't push themselves. When they have a task that is not inspected or measured, they will not push themselves to do it well. They will conclude that the task is not important.

For those of you who are expert leaders, assess if this style is working for your team. If so, great!

If your team is not performing, are you open to adopting a warm demander leader style? If so, do the following:

- Address your low warmth:

  - Ask yourself about each of your team members. Specifically what do you know about them personally?

  - Meet with each team member individually for thirty minutes for coffee to have a **Get-to-Know-You Conversation** where you each share with each other what you do for fun and what you are working on.

  - Take note of each of your team members' joys (what they do for fun) and what each person is working on (their personal and professional goals).

  - Commit to building and maintaining personal relationships with each of your team members.

  - Schedule periodic follow-up check-ins with each of your team members when you set aside the routine work discussions and catch up on each other's personal lives and goals (maybe monthly, quarterly).

  - Consider having the check-in venue be somewhere other than your office to help distinguish it from routine work discussions.

- Address being a low demander:

  - For each of your team members, ask yourself how they are performing against what you have asked them to do (their key activities). Then define how you need them to perform for your team to win.

  - Ask yourself how you are monitoring your team's performance and providing timely feedback to them. If you do not have an acceptable method in place, establish how you will operationalize your expectations. An effective way is to **set up regular forums** where you review the performance of activities and align on actions needed to address risks and issues.

GET-TO-KNOW-YOU CONVERSATION 30 MINUTES

ASK AND SHARE YOUR ANSWERS

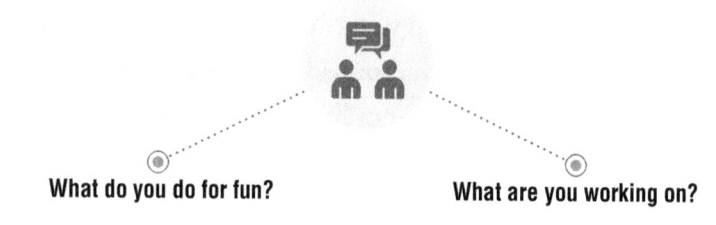

What do you do for fun?

What are you working on?

USE 10-10-10 FORMAT

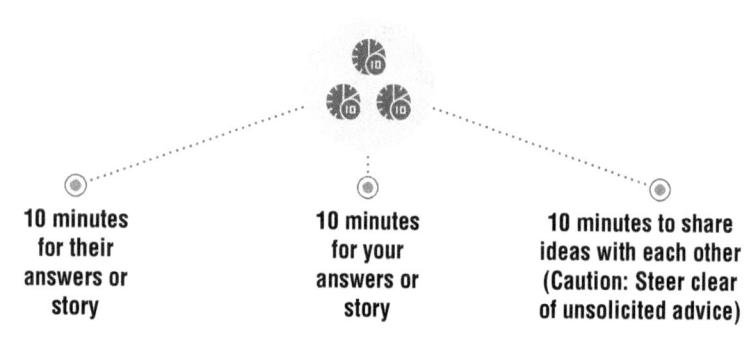

10 minutes for their answers or story

10 minutes for your answers or story

10 minutes to share ideas with each other (Caution: Steer clear of unsolicited advice)

MODEL EXCELLENT SOCIAL SKILLS

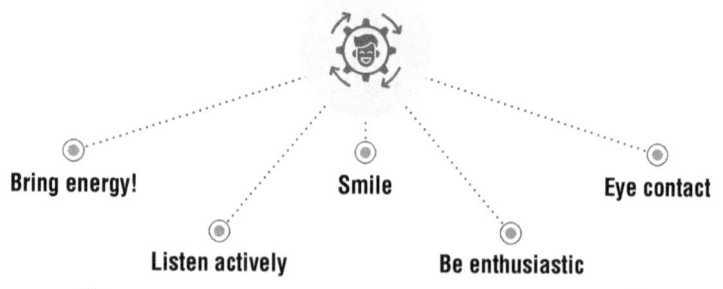

Bring energy!

Smile

Eye contact

Listen actively

Be enthusiastic

 BE INTERESTED and BE INTERESTING

SET UP YOUR FORUMS AND LET THEM RUN

KEY ACTIVITIES

Make a list of your team members' key activities.

DEFINE GOOD

Spell out, by activity what good is. Also describe excellent and poor.

ESTABLISH METRICS

Figure out how you will measure performance for each activity.

SET UP FORUMS

Set up regular meetings or forums to review the performance of activities and to determine actions needed to address risks and issues.

How to operationalize your expectations

FOUR

THE DRIVER

Stop Doing Everything That You're Doing

I took over this engineering group. It was a big group of like thirty people. Their purpose was to drive improvement in the quality of the products. They were so frantically busy that they were missing their kids' softball games. This story from Dave S., the tech exec.

I met with each person and asked each one a question that had three possible answers. "You're really busy doing all this stuff. How is the quality of the product you're working on?" The answer was either getting better, getting worse, or staying the same.

Every single person said, "Staying the same or getting worse."

I got them all together and told them to stop doing everything they were doing. Only do these three things (address outages, minor configuration changes, basic maintenance)—nothing else. No extra projects.

They just blew up. They said things like their business partners will get mad. I literally had one guy yelling. I replied, "You told me everything you do was not working. Every single one of you said what you're doing is not improving quality or actually it's making it worse. So you're going to stop doing it."

I said, "This isn't up for debate. You're going to stop. If anybody that you're working with has a problem, send them to me."

They stopped. No one complained. Because what they had been doing wasn't working. This change gave us time to work on the operating model.

About three months later, after we got the operating model in place and working, three things happened:

- They were able to get to their kids' softball games.
- The quality of the product got better because they were doing the right stuff.
- Employee engagement of that group went from the lowest in the company to the highest in the company.

It was such a dramatic change that my boss and the head of HR came to me and said, "What did you do?"

I told them I defined how they should operate, how they should develop, and how they could be successful. So many people don't get that in the workplace. How often did anybody sit down and say to you, "This is how we're going to operate? And this is what I want you to do. And this is what I don't want you to do."

I don't think that's ever happened to me. Ever. It's where I start with my teams.

Cold Calling Kid

My dad started his own company, which was like a sales organization when I was probably in third or fourth grade. I talked a lot then and I was a bit argumentative, said Eric K., an entrepreneur and professor.

Dad was getting it going and he brought me in to help him. I would do projects around his office and then at one point, he decided to put me on the phone. This was pre-internet days. I was helping build lists for him.

I was basically cold calling companies and trying to get them to talk to me so I could get information from them that my dad wanted. And I vividly remember when I would call people in the South, often there would be a receptionist. They would regularly answer my questions by saying "Yes, ma'am" or "No, ma'am" to me.

My voice hadn't changed yet. It bothered me that the receptionist thought I was a female. So I didn't want to make the calls, but I still did it because my dad forced me to.

What happened was I learned a lot about just being comfortable talking to people and not caring what people thought. It was a powerful experience and gave me really good insight early on. I wouldn't have had that experience if my dad hadn't forced me to try something I hadn't done before and forced me to stick with it.

THE DRIVER

The driver is a leader that sets high goals for their team members and is quick to express displeasure when their expectations are not met. Often, the driver rules by fear of retribution and can be cruel. They exude absolute power over the team and do not seek or value new ideas or feedback from the team.

Dave's assessment of his new team revealed a total reset was needed. Predictably, his team resisted. Being the boss, he was able to declare, "This isn't negotiable." He took the heat from them and pushed them where they needed to go to improve.

Eric's dad had a driver style too. He wasn't cruel, but he was firm. Eric knew he had to finish the job his dad assigned, so he muscled through it. Because of that experience that he would have preferred to avoid, he grew.

When the driver leader sets goals, they expect them to be met. When goals are not met, someone will bear the brunt of their displeasure. When goals are met, higher goals will be set.

The driver's conversations with team members often are limited to work topics only. They push for progress. Team members who perform well for them are those who like goals and clearly defined work assignments that do not require problem solving or collaboration.

Many of today's early career employees will not be all in for a driver leader who shows low warmth and high demand. They will appreciate clearly defined goals set by their manager. However, when they struggle with a task, many will not ask for help from a leader who is not warm enough. Instead, they will avoid the task. They will call in sick to work. They may even quit their job.

For those of you who are driver leaders, assess if this style is working for your team. If so, great! If your team is not performing, are you open to adopting a warm demander leader style? If so, do the following:

- Continue being a high demander:
  - Know that you are doing a good job establishing and monitoring your team members' goals. Keep this up.

- Address your low warmth:
  - Ask yourself about each of your team members, specifically what do you know about them personally.

  - Meet with each team member individually for thirty minutes for coffee to have a **Get-to-Know-You Conversation** where you each share with each other what you do for fun and what you are working on.

  - Take note of each of your team members' joys (what they do for fun) and what each person is working on (their personal and professional goals).

  - Commit to building and maintaining personal relationships with each of your team members.

  - Schedule periodic follow-up check-ins with each of your team members when you set aside the routine work discussions and catch up on each others' personal lives and goals (monthly, quarterly).

  - Consider having the check-in venue being somewhere other than your office to help distinguish it from routine work discussions.

GET-TO-KNOW-YOU CONVERSATION 30 MINUTES

ASK AND SHARE YOUR ANSWERS

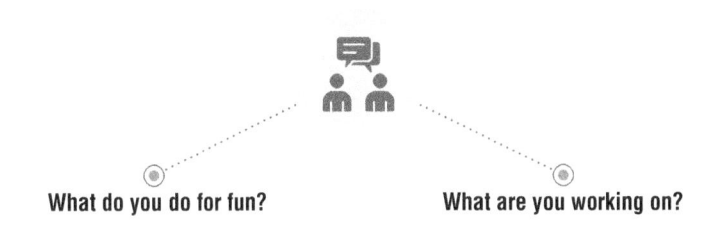

What do you do for fun?   What are you working on?

USE 10-10-10 FORMAT

| 10 minutes for their answers or story | 10 minutes for your answers or story | 10 minutes to share ideas with each other (Caution: Steer clear of unsolicited advice) |

MODEL EXCELLENT SOCIAL SKILLS

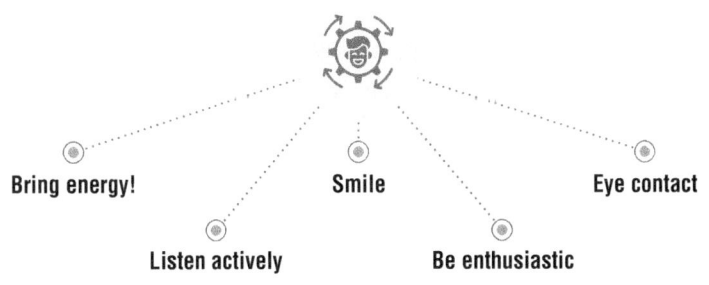

Bring energy!   Smile   Eye contact

Listen actively   Be enthusiastic

BE INTERESTED and BE INTERESTING

FIVE

THE BUDDY

Crap Sandwich

I don't do a very good job at giving feedback to someone who is underperforming, I am the softie. In some instances, I let things slide. I am better at it now, said Kevin L., partner in a law firm.

People talk about the crap sandwich approach. You say something nice, give criticism, say something else nice. People say that's terribly ineffective and the worst thing you could possibly do. I would do that all the time. I still do it. But not as often.

There was a member of my team, a decent performer, and I hope she is doing fine now. But she did something, and it didn't go well. It wasn't disastrous, but she hadn't done a good job. I did that with her, I gave her a crap sandwich.

When I did this, she said, "I really appreciate that. That's why I like working with you because you don't get mad when I screw up."

Hearing that from her made me feel like I had just screwed up. It was clear I had not been effective. I was trying to convey that she had done a bad job.

Talkative Boss

I worked for Mike for about three years. He was my direct manager, said Andy K., director of a consumer products goods company. Mike's the type of guy that likes to talk. It was just in his nature to hear himself talk.

It created a condition that was easier for me as a relatively new person to feel comfortable sharing my thoughts, frustrations, and observations. I remember saying things like, "Man, like, this is messed up. I can't believe we're doing it this way. This is like ten years behind the industry."

He created the right conditions that made me able to open up and have those conversations. When I was talking about the work I was doing, my career goals and all this kind of stuff, he shared an observation and gave me advice that stuck with me. He said there are people that can work ten years in a job and get five years of experience. They just kind of show up and go through the motions and just sort of fight through it.

Then there are people that can work five years in a job and get ten years of experience. If you're really intentional about it, this can be you, and it doesn't mean you have to work eighty hours a week. It means you've got to approach each meeting, each engagement, and each initiative as an opportunity to learn and better yourself. If you take that mindset, that's how you can accelerate your career.

This inspired a mindset shift. His well-timed advice really resonated with me. He helped me transition from a functional role by giving me opportunities to build new skills. I used to be in what we call process development, which is more of a laboratory-based role. Then I moved into project management. I expressed an interest in it and then he helped build off that interest by challenging me and saying, "Hey, you know, I want you to lead this project, or I want you to do that."

He helped me take it from my passive interest by saying, "You should do this. Go run with it."

THE BUDDY

The buddy is a leader who has strong personal relationships with their team members. The buddy doesn't push their team members to meet goals or reprimand them for their mistakes. Like Kevin, they struggle with giving direct feedback to a team member who has messed up. Instead the buddy leader relies on their team members to push themselves with their own goals and to catch, acknowledge, and address their mistakes.

Often, the buddy leader collaborates with their team members on tasks or encourages them to work with others to innovate and solve problems. They are supportive of new ideas and approaches to improvement. They inspire team building.

Like Mike, Andy's boss, they are approachable. When solicited, a buddy leader is quick to offer advice and share what's worked for them. They are all about their team members and want them to grow and develop.

Buddy leaders spend time getting to know each team member and keep tabs on their personal lives. Additionally, they share their personal lives with their team members. They view their team members as friends or family members.

With high warmth and low demand, these bosses are easygoing.

Team members who perform well for them are those who like to experiment with different options before determining a solution, and those who like to work at their own pace. Many of today's early career employees will not be all in for a buddy leader. They will appreciate the relationship they build with their manager.

When they have a task that is not inspected or measured, they will not push themselves to do it well. Without the feedback, they will conclude that the task is not important.

For those of you who are buddy leaders, assess if this style is working for your team. If so, great! If your team is not performing, are you open to adopting a warm demander leader style? If so, do the following.

- Continue being high warmth: You are doing a great job establishing and maintaining personal relationships with your team members. Keep this up.

- Address being a low demander:

  - For each of your team members, ask yourself how they are performing against what you have asked them to do (their key activities). Then define how you need them to perform for your team to win.

  - Ask yourself how you are monitoring your team's performance and providing timely feedback to them. If you do not have an acceptable method in place, establish how you will operationalize your expectations. An effective way is to **set up regular forums** where you review the performance of activities and align on actions needed to address risks and issues.

SET UP YOUR FORUMS
AND LET THEM RUN

KEY ACTIVITIES

Make a list of your team members' key activities.

DEFINE GOOD

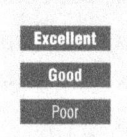

Spell out, by activity what good is. Also describe excellent and poor.

ESTABLISH METRICS

Figure out how you will measure performance for each activity.

SET UP FORUMS

Set up regular meetings or forums to review the performance of activities and to determine actions needed to address risks and issues.

How to operationalize your expectations

SIX

THE WARM DEMANDER

Treated Me Like a Partner

Early in my career, my bank merged with another bank, said Lori I., a strategic adviser and transformation leader. I was given a stretch opportunity, working with an executive I had never met. His name was Stan. He was the new leader of the commercial bank for the Midwest region.

My job was to help Stan figure out how to be successful in the market. This work included integrating the two organizations. Stan set me up to lead this effort. He invited me to all the meetings with all the senior-level people. He introduced me, and he endorsed me.

Stan was a straight shooter. He had no real agenda. He had a casual openness. He would say what he thought regardless of who you were, whether you were a junior person like me or the CEO. I saw him have hard conversations including with the CEO. And when there were hard conversations that happened outside of my presence, he filled me in on them. Stan didn't treat me as an underling. He treated me like a partner. He was vulnerable and real with me, and that made it possible for me to be the same with him.

Stan introduced me to senior leaders and told them I was going to work with them to figure out how their organizations needed to change to support the merger. He endorsed me upfront and all along the way. I could feel that he had my back. This gave me the confidence to facilitate and negotiate. I was able to bring people together from different parts of the company and get the merged company's new ways of working established and in place. As a result, the company's success in the marketplace grew.

Later when I worked with other leaders, who were less skilled than Stan, I was better able to appreciate what an extraordinary experience I had had working with him and how it had impacted me.

Stan had implicitly valued my expertise and skills. He demonstrated he trusted me, and I was able to be 100 percent real with him. From the onset, I had a sense of belonging and that propelled me forward to confidently get our banks integrated.

Off to the Board Meeting

My first boss who really invested in me was a guy who was the comptroller of a small public company, said Eric K., the entrepreneur and professor. The company eventually sold for $3.5 billion.

His name was Dan. He offered me a job as a staff accountant even though he knew I didn't want to be an accountant forever. He hired me because I had a set of skills that were really good, and I was a hard worker.

He would push me to do different things all the time. He'd say "try this" and "what about that." He really put me in different positions. And that really was helpful for me. I was pretty early in my career. So I was junior. We were a company that was growing fairly fast. We were trying to figure out how to use all these data we had about sales and stuff.

One of the big things I did was put together the Daily Sales Report. It went out to all the senior executives and the board. One time there was some kind of an issue with the board, and they were going to have an important board meeting to discuss it. There was a question that they had about something on the Daily Sales Report. They reached out to Dan and said we need this answer. They said this board meeting is coming up, can you come talk to us about this?

Dan made a choice right there. He said, "You should have Eric come. Eric is the one who knows these reports."

Basically, he put me in front of these people, and I think that was one of those situations where I really grew. He demonstrated that he had confidence in me. I think that type of thing was his MO and why I liked working with him. He saw something in me and knew that having me do more would help me as well as help him.

THE WARM DEMANDER

The warm demander works to establish rapport with each team member. They seek to understand their team members and inspire them to engage in challenging work.

Lori sensed Stan's confidence in himself and in her by how he operated. His casual openness and formal endorsement of her made it easier for Lori to step into the challenging job she was handpicked to do. She knew Stan had her back.

Warm demander leaders push their team members to extend themselves beyond what the team member is comfortable with in order for them to grow. Often, the warm demander leader asks the team member to take a leap of faith and do assignments or tasks that they would never have considered on their own.

> Warm demander leaders encourage their team members by saying phrases like this:
> - You are the right person for this job.
> - I believe in you.
> - You got this.
> - I am right here for you.

Dan's choice to have Eric go to their board to answer the questions about the Daily Sales Report demonstrated to the board what Eric could sense when Dan told him he was going to the board meeting. With that choice, Dan conveyed these messages:

Eric knows his stuff.

Eric can answer your questions.

I trust Eric.

Eric is ready for more.

I've got Eric's back.

The team member trusts the warm demander because of their relationship. The team member will grow in skills and confidence often exceeding their own expectations of what's possible because of their warm demander leader who is high in warmth and high in demand.

The warm demander leader is a person everyone wants to be around because they are positive and confident. Their team members want to please them because they like and trust them and for this reason are willing to be pushed to do extraordinary things.

Warm demander leaders develop winners.

Team members who perform well for warm demanders are those who find value in personal connection and being part of a team that collaborates and supports each other to grow and achieve.

Today's early career employees will be all in for the warm demander leader. They need to feel their manager is genuinely interested in their success. When they trust their manager, they will respond positively when their manager pushes them to take on new assignments. Also when they have a task that they know will be inspected or measured, they will push themselves to do it well.

They will win. You will win—and it will be fun.

For those of you who are warm demanders, high-five! Consider ways you can have your awesomeness infiltrate other parts of your organization.

- Put your hand up to lead the teams of early career employees that are the most important to your company's bottom line or future.

- Arm yourself with the Be-Social Method and transform your teams into high-performing all stars.

- Mentor another leader or two who is looking to transform into a warm demander leader.

My Warm Demander Teacher

I was born in the Bahamas, said Patricia G., a senior associate dean at a research university. My family moved to Brooklyn. I spent kindergarten, first grade, second grade, and one day of the third grade at one school. Then, after the first day of third grade, my family moved to another part of Brooklyn, and on the second day of third grade, I started in a second school.

I was uncertain of how I would be received, being the new student. I was fond of my old school where I knew everyone and was in the gifted and talented classroom. At my new school, I was not placed in the gifted and talented classroom.

My first day there, my new teacher greeted me. Her name was Mrs. Ethel Hirschman. She was a very warm and welcoming person. She was kind and made me feel like I found a home—which was good because I was very worried about making the switch from one school where I knew everyone to another one where I didn't know anyone.

Something about our interactions made her push my principal to have me retested. Mrs. Hirschman could see I needed to be challenged more than I was. She was very involved in the process to have me retested, which our principal resisted at first.

After the testing, instead of changing me to the gifted and talented classroom, the principal had me go into the fourth grade for reading and math. And then when I started fourth grade, I was placed in the gifted and talented classroom.

Later when I was in middle school and Mrs. Hirschman was teaching kindergarten, she had me come to her classroom at least once a day to help her teach reading to her students.

We stayed in touch in middle school and even beyond that. Mrs. Hirschman gave her attention and support to me and other students who needed assistance. She pushed us. Her style made an impact on me.

Today, I am especially grateful to be in a job where I push to get individual students the attention and the support they need. Because I know firsthand what a difference it makes.

My Warm Demander Dad

My dad was probably the biggest role model in my life when I was young, Bob G., a retired financial services executive, remembers.

My dad finished high school, but he did not go to college. He was a painter. In fact, he painted the ceilings in the Drake Hotel in Chicago. He told me that he would see businesspeople coming into the Drake with their suits on when they were checking into the hotel. When he saw this, he said to himself, "I want to do that, I don't want to be up on the scaffolding painting, I want to be a businessperson."

Plus, the paint fumes were starting to concern him. He was concerned about the impact of the fumes on his health. So he made a change. He got into insurance.

My dad was a person who had a good personality. He liked people. He was always a flashy dresser like the typical insurance salesman. He could have sold used cars too. He was really successful. He became a staff manager. He had ten people working for him. He would go out with them and train them and help them.

I felt, with me, he was tough. He expected me to do well in school. But he was a very warm individual and I always felt like I could talk to him. I probably didn't take advantage of it as much as I should have.

One of my regrets in life is, when he died, and when he was dying, I really didn't tell him how much of an influence he had on my life.

A lot of my ideas for how to build my sales organization in the bank I got from my dad because he was a sales manager. He knew what made salespeople tick, what kind of people are good for sales, what kind of incentive program you need to have to make it work. And I think it just helped me with that mentality. Whereas most of the people at the bank, at least at that time, didn't have the sales mentality.

I met my dad's friends, his coworkers, and I knew what kind of people they were. They were very gregarious and outgoing. My dad used to bring these numbers home. Every week he'd bring a sheet home, his sheet that ranked all these guys including himself, as the staff manager. The sheet showed you exactly where you stood.

I remember when I was really small, my dad would come home for dinner. Then he would leave to go out because he made his sales calls at night. He'd be leaving at sixish in the evening, and I would say, "Dad why do you have to go to work?" and he would say, "So you can go to college."

I'll never forget that. So I knew I had to go to college. He was really proud of my education.

My Warm Demander Mom and Uncle

I grew up in a rough area of New Jersey, where I was part of an immigrant family. This is Manny's story. You met Manny earlier. He is now director of a multinational mass media and entertainment company.

My mother was always my mentor, my teacher, my best friend, and my counselor. She was just a strong-willed lady. She was very tough, very fair, very loving, which my brother and I needed at that time.

My uncle treated me as his golden boy. My uncle would say, "There's no way Manny did that. Somebody else did." He was like the cheerleader with a biased opinion of what was going on. I needed that because unfortunately my dad was in and out of my life.

The odds are stacked against you when you grow up in an urban Hispanic ghetto, like I did, in New Jersey. My education was not at the caliber of what kids like my own children have, who are growing up in a suburb of Chicago. I was the oldest in my family. I was going to be the first one to go to college. I just wanted to get out of the hood.

When I was about thirteen, everything started to take shape like a large mountain that I would need to climb. During that period of time, I said to my mom, "You know what, this is kind of insurmountable. I'm just going to do the best I can and maybe end up just being a mechanic."

My mother's response was, "Absolutely not. I did not sacrifice my own life for that. More importantly, you have talents and gifts that a lot of people don't have, and you would be wasting them. And I'm not going to allow that to happen."

My uncle stepped in as well. And he said, "What are you, nuts? We work in factories. That's not for you. That's not for your brother, your cousins. Don't worry about it. We're gonna help you however we can."

They stepped up and supported me during my college years at Notre Dame. When you show up freshman year of college, there is a vast difference in preparedness for college and resources between kids who grew up how I did in an urban Hispanic ghetto of New Jersey and kids who grew up in an affluent suburb of Chicago, like my children are. Having the emotional support of my mother and uncle carried me through.

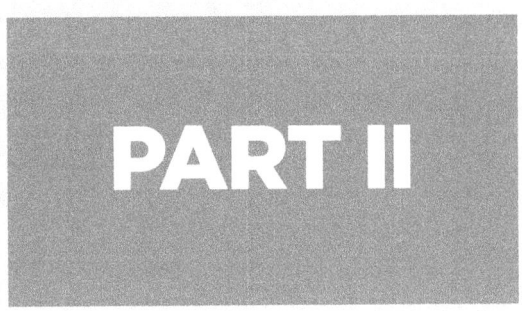

PART II

You are either someone who has a network of people who support, encourage, and inspire each other, or someone who does not but most likely could benefit from such a network.

Chances are if you are part of that second group, you could figure out a way to grow and evolve your network if you wanted to.

In other words, you don't need someone to "teach" business networking practices to you. This is because, most likely, you have grown up being pushed to meet people, to get to know people, and to connect people and ask for help.

You might just be a little rusty, but with effort you could make it happen.

To me, this quote attributed to Epicurus clearly says why each of us should do the work of building and maintaining a network of people who support, encourage, and inspire each other (and encourage those we lead to do the same).

> "It is not so much our friends' help that helps us, as the confident knowledge that they will help us."
> —Epicurus

Many Gen Zers were not pushed to master the social practices that lead to a group of friends who stick by you through thick and thin. When they were growing up, rather than having unstructured time in real life with friends where these skills are honed, they spent a lot of time online. As a result, these young adults are showing up at work with some key soft skills weaknesses that are frustrating their managers.

This is where you come in. You can warmly demand they demonstrate relationship building practices as part of their job. In other words, you can "teach" social practices to your Gen Z team members. The Be-Social Method introduced in this part of the book gives you a simple framework so that you can intentionally model relationship building to your team members.

Also the Be-Social Method is a fresh new way you can think about relationship building. For your early career team member, it will probably be the first time they think purposefully about building and maintaining a professional network. You will help them understand that doing this work will make them better at their job and help them in their career. BONUS: I think you are going to like it for yourself, too.

In Part II, you get an overview of the Be-Social Method. Learning this method will give you the anchor you need for coaching your team members on how to strengthen key soft skills they need to perform better in the job.

SEVEN

THE BE-SOCIAL METHOD

Friends at Work

I know these young people hate it, but I think you need face time. So says Kelly R., a former supervisor for the US probation office.

I was a federal probation officer for over twenty years, and I had several workplace friends. You have to have relationships with coworkers. You have to know about each other's personal lives, not intensely, but about their family. So that you know if they are struggling because they're dealing with a sick kid or something else. You need human relationships.

People you work with need to feel like they can talk to you, and I just don't think you get that over Zoom. You need a foundation first. I think once you have a foundation, then you can go to Zoom.

Young adults today who are working virtually, they think Zoom is great. I think it's horrible. But they don't know it. They don't know anything else. They are missing the development of relationships with their boss and their coworkers and the development of their social skills.

We were in the office when I was a young adult. My boss knew the basics of me. I felt like I couldn't ask him much. He was more private than I was. Being in the office, I formed personal relationships with my coworkers. We got to know each other by going out to lunch and going out for drinks. That's how you get to know people. The people who did the best were the ones who had built those relationships.

When I became a supervisor, I knew that. The ones I kept my eyes on were the ones who stayed in their office and didn't go to lunch with people or out for a drink. I knew those were the ones who were going to struggle because our work is stressful, and you need to be able to vent and have that support system. If you don't do that, you are going to be in a world of hurt.

We had deadlines that were stressful and the pressure of listening to lives in crisis was part of our job. As a federal probation officer, you are the recipient of sad, sad stories. The information is confidential so you can't bring it home. But you can talk about it with coworkers. Plus, you really need to have a circle of colleagues to bounce things off just to get the work done. There were so many variations to our work. Those with experience were a wealth of knowledge and could help you save time by pointing you in the right direction.

You needed that base knowledge to leverage in order to get your work done in a timely manner. Otherwise, you were reinventing the wheel, which took longer. Also, the stress of being in court was something we all shared. You had people you could share your experience with, so you didn't feel like you were the only one who experienced the attorney who was an ass. You didn't feel like it's just me, you realized he's an ass to everybody.

Someone would say, "He was mean to you?" and I'd say, "Oh yeah!" It puts a whole different perspective on it. You don't feel like you are so crappy at your job. Without that chance to share, you would internalize the encounter and think you are doing a bad job.

THE BE-SOCIAL METHOD

The Be-Social Method is a fresh, straightforward approach that, once embraced, results in your having a professional network of people who support, encourage, and inspire each other.

In 2009, after losing my job, I realized there were literally only two people who knew what I did professionally. I had let my professional network atrophy. Because of this, I did a tremendous amount of work to rebuild my network. After that, I vowed to myself that I would never find myself without a professional network again.

I embraced professional networking with a fury.

I tried all kinds of networking practices. So much so that my friends started introducing me as, "This is Colleen McFarland. She's an excellent networker." My colleagues at Centric Consulting asked me to put a workshop together for them on networking. After I did this, they asked me to offer the workshop to our whole company, which I did.

HOW WRIGLEY FIELD MADE ME A BETTER NETWORKER

After creating the networking workshop for my colleagues, I found a home for it at the Career Transition Center in Chicago. I branded the workshop, "How Wrigley Field Made Me a Better Networker" (and I explain this in more depth in chapter 8). My approach I call the Be-Social Method. I have been delivering the workshops two or three times a year ever since. Currently, the workshops are a series of five one-hour webinars. They're so much fun.

What also happened during this time is that I went through a personal transformation.

I went from having a **low social battery** to
→ Having **lots of energy**

From being **timid** meeting new people to
→ Being completely **at ease**

From viewing networking as **daunting** to
→ Having **confidence** in my skills

From seeing networking as **transactional** to
→ Seeing it as **growing relationships**

From thinking of networking as **painful** to
→ Being **full of joy when I see people**

Humans need each other more than we realize sometimes. You as a leader can encourage and push your team members to develop social skills that help them to connect, collaborate, support, and inspire each other.

I have developed the Be-Social Method and have refined it over ten years as I delivered it in my workshops. It is transformative. Use the Be-Social Method to ignite in your employees the desire to build workplace relationships.

My workshop participants say it best:

- *Since I've embraced the Be-Social Method, I have lots of energy.*

- *I am more at ease when talking with anyone.*

- *I see the Be-Social practices as a holistic way to build and maintain relationships, not singularly as transactions.*

- *Networking the Be-Social way is joyful!*

THE BE-SOCIAL BUILDING BLOCKS

Those of us who can remember a time before the internet most likely were forced to develop social skills by our parents, extended family, friends, teachers, coaches, and neighbors.

As a child in the 1970s before anyone had a smartphone or even a personal computer, I was expected to greet adults and engage in small talk with them. I also was required to answer our family telephone land line, having no idea who was going to be at the other end of the phone, by stating my name as my greeting.

My Catholic grade school was always having us students fundraise by selling something to our neighbors and extended family. I remember ringing doorbells and making phone calls selling magazine subscriptions and boxes of chocolate. Also, it was not unusual for my mother to send me to a neighbor's house to deliver something or pick up something, during which time I was required to make eye contact, smile, speak, and be polite.

I don't remember not wanting to do this. But my guess is there were some neighbors whose doorbells I was more comfortable ringing than others. Plus, we were sent outside to "go play," which meant go find some neighborhood kids, make up some games, and don't come home for at least two hours, preferably three.

I developed social skills through those forced activities. Also, I got to know people and I had the potential to know others through those relationships.

BUILDING BLOCK: CURRENT AND POTENTIAL NETWORK FRAMEWORK

The first building block for the Be-Social network is the **Current & Potential Network** framework for how to think about "your people." It is represented by four concentric circles.

─ CURRENT & POTENTIAL NETWORK ─

 CURRENT NETWORK

KNOW AND CURRENT

Caught up with in a real way.
*Know what each other
is working on.*

KNOW AND NOT CURRENT

You were *"close"* before
but are not caught up now
or you were never *"close."*

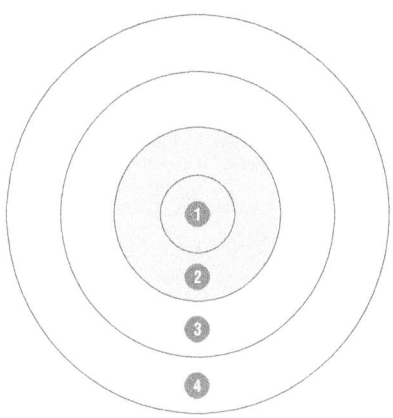

 POTENTIAL NETWORK

EASY TO KNOW

People you see
or could see.
They are in your path.

WANT TO KNOW

People you need
a plan to meet.
They are not in your path.

**The current and potential network framework,
the first building block of the Be-Social network**

Know and Current: The inner circle represents the people you know and are current with. These are the people that you are caught up with in a real way. You have had a meaningful conversation recently with them. They could repeat to someone what you are working on and what you do for fun.

Similarly, you could share with someone else what each person in your inner circle is working on and what they do for fun.

Know and Not Current: The second circle goes around the inner circle. It represents people that you know but are not current with. You have met. You know each other's names. These are people either that you once were close to but it's been a while since you caught up, or these are people that you have met and know but have never had a meaningful conversation with.

You have no idea what they currently do for fun or what they are working on, and, similarly, they know very little about what is going on with you.

These two circles represent your current network of support.

Your potential network of support is two additional groups.

Easy to Know: The third circle goes around the current network of support, and it represents people who are easy for you to know. These are people that you literally see or could see without much effort. They are on your path.

They can be neighbors, people you see in your grocery store, your gym, your church, your child's school, or at work. You could meet them by simply introducing yourself or arranging for a friend to introduce you.

Want to Know: The fourth circle is the outer circle, and it represents people you want to know. People in this group can be people you believe could help you with what you are working on. They can also be people you think would be fun to know. You may know their name, like your favorite pro baseball player, or you may just have a general description of them, like someone who has been to Antarctica in the past year. Since they are not on your path, you need a plan to meet them.

Relationship building begins with taking stock of your network and considering who you would like to add to your network. Use this framework to help you identify "your people."

BUILDING BLOCK: BE CURIOUS & READY TO SHARE

The second building block of the Be-Social Method is to **Be Curious & Ready to Share**.

> The key to successful networking is
> to be INTERESTED and to be INTERESTING.

When I began working on professional networking, I struggled with what came after being introduced to someone. Many people call this small talk. Through trial and error, I came up with the best two questions to ask in these situations.

These two questions make having conversations with people I meet or am catching up with a breeze.

> Two Questions to Ask:
> What do you do for fun?
> What are you working on?

I love asking these questions because the person I am asking often shares something interesting.

What do you do for fun? Just this month, someone told me he likes to test out gaming apps on Roblox. Another person told me about the summer concerts she was planning to attend and her insider tip for getting good tickets. Another person filled me in on the SS *Badger* four-hour ferry boat she likes to take across Lake Michigan.

I share what I am doing for fun too. Which lately has been a lot of biking. I tell how I did my first organized ride this year, the Five Boro Bike Tour in New York City. I've had a blast sharing this with people and answering their questions about the ride and encouraging them to tell their bike-riding friends to check it out.

What are you working on? When you ask someone what they are working on, it gives them a chance to tell you either a personal goal like preparing to go on a vacation or looking for childcare for their newborn baby, or a professional goal like landing their next big deal or finding a new job.

When I learn what someone is working on, I can consider how my network could help them out. Sometimes I can immediately offer to connect them to someone or share a resource with them. Other times I will think of some ideas later. When this happens, it gives me a purposeful reason to reach out to them.

Similarly, when I share with them what I am working on, I give them the opportunity to consider any information they have that could help me out, and consider who they know that they think I should meet.

See how asking these two questions works? Using them can work for you too. So try them out.

When we exchange with each other what we do for fun and what we are working on, it shows we are interested in getting to know each other personally. Plus, it's interesting and makes the conversation more memorable.

BUILDING BLOCK: JOYS YOU EMBRACE OR WILL EMBRACE

The third building block of the Be-Social Method is joys you embrace or will embrace. Sharing what you do for fun comes from knowing your joys.

Curate joys in your life and carve out time to do them. In my workshops, people have shared several joys including music, learning, books, piano, dogs, their children, writing, running, and traveling.

I have had people in my workshops who have not been able to name anything in their life that currently brings them joy. To them, I give the assignment to name at least one joy they would like to embrace since joys are critical for our well-being.

When we partake in joyous activities, we counteract the daily stresses of life. We need to smile every day, and for some of us that's going to mean scheduling time to do things we enjoy.

We also use our joys for building and maintaining our personal network. When I began working on professional networking, I tried a lot of different ways to meet and get to know people.

What I found out through trial and error was this:

- Networking takes time and I needed to be selective which activities I added.

- I had more success meeting people when I did activities that brought me joy or when I added networking practices to activities (like attending my children's baseball or hockey games) that I was already doing.

EIGHT

THE BE-SOCIAL METHOD NETWORKING PRACTICES

One of my joys is going to Chicago Cubs baseball games at Wrigley Field. I love going to weekday afternoon games. Let me share this story.

One Friday in July 2011, I arrived around 11:30 a.m. at an establishment outside of Wrigley Field. My job was to go early and hold a table for my friends who were going to join me for lunch and a game. When I arrived, I ordered a beverage. As I was drinking the beverage, I noticed that other people at the establishment were doing the same thing. We were "the table holders." Then I noticed that as these people's guests were arriving, they were introducing them to each other.

I thought this was odd. I wondered who would agree to go to lunch and a Cubs game with people they didn't know. Then I realized that I would do that! I loved Chicago Cubs ball games, and I would love to meet people who also enjoyed going to Cubs games.

I decided right then and there that I was going to start bringing people together who didn't know each other for lunch and a Cubs game. I began that practice the next season and have been doing it ever since.

My format is simple. I invite three people who I think would benefit from getting to know each other, to lunch and a game. At lunch, I ask them to share a bit of their story with each other including what they do for fun, what they are working on, and who they'd like to meet. From there, the conversation flows.

NETWORKING THROUGH OUR JOYS

Through our joys we can work on the practices that are essential for building and maintaining a network. Consider how you can use one of your joys to connect people by organizing an event.

Connecting people is one of the sets of the networking practices that are part of the Be-Social Method. The networking practices are the final building block of the Be-Social Method.

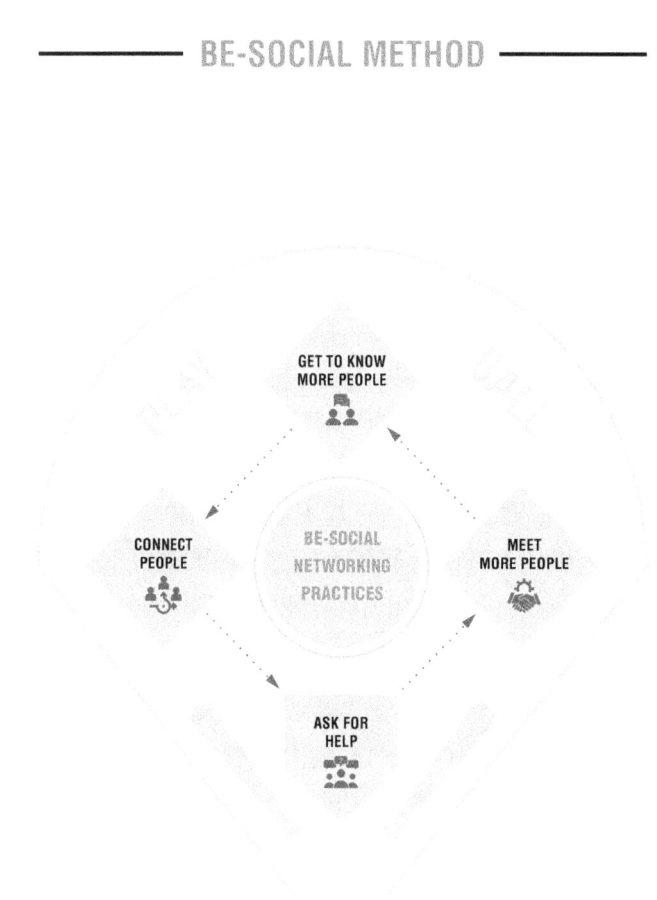

**The Be-Social Method for networking.
Think of the networking practices like a baseball diamond.**

MEET MORE PEOPLE

The first set of practices are those related to meeting more people.

Meet More People Practices are these:

- ☐ Introduce yourself to someone you don't know at a party/event or when out and about.
- ☐ Ask people you meet about their work/profession.
- ☐ Engage with people on social media (LinkedIn, Facebook, Instagram, or X) to meet them.
- ☐ Attend larger (more than ten people) networking events put on by others.
- ☐ Participate in formal organizations (professional, charitable, hobby, special interest, religious, or political groups), or work on a passion project or side gig.

Each Saturday morning, I have made it my habit to stop and consider who I have met that week. Then I request to connect with my new contacts on LinkedIn. For you this could be Facebook, Instagram, or X. By doing this weekly, I avoid being in the awkward position of reaching out to connect with someone when I need something from them.

GET TO KNOW MORE PEOPLE

The second set of practices are those related to getting to know more people. Many of these practices also work for catching up with someone you have lost touch with (for example, a former work colleague, high school friend, or neighbor).

Get to Know More People Practices are these:

- ☐ Exchange "elevator speeches" and stories.
- ☐ Join an organization (professional, charitable, hobby or special interest, religious, political) and lead a group such as a committee.
- ☐ Invite someone to network over coffee/video call (less than thirty minutes).
- ☐ Invite someone to network over lunch/drinks/dinner (one hour plus).
- ☐ Engage digitally with someone to get to know them via extended chat or text.

I have found when I have a thirty-minute coffee or video chat with someone I am getting to know, keeping in mind the 10-10-10 format is magical. The 10-10-10 format is splitting the conversation into three chapters, each chapter takes less than ten minutes.

Begin the networking conversation by setting the structure for the conversation by following this script. After you thank the person for their time say this:

Your story (<10 minutes)
"I'd like to start with you. I want to hear your story. What are you working on? What are you doing these days for fun?"

My story (<10 minutes)
"Then, I'd like to share my story with you."

Advice (<10 minutes)
"Lastly, I'd love to hear any advice you have for me."

With the 10-10-10 format, you give the conversation structure, which is needed when you have limited time to connect with someone. I have found people truly appreciate my doing the work of facilitating the conversation so it's productive. You will too.

CONNECT PEOPLE

The third set of practices are those related to connecting people. I have found by doing the *Connect People Practices*, I am inspired to do the practices of meeting and getting to know people, since those practices result in me having new people to connect each year.

Connect People Practices are these:

- ☐ Introduce people to each other at events/meetings.
- ☐ Introduce people to each other over email or text (five-minute favor).
- ☐ Spend time considering who you connect and why.
- ☐ Introduce a small group (two or three people) to each other at an event hosted by you.
- ☐ Host a large event for four or more people to meet or reconnect with others.

I encourage you to establish a signature event for yourself. Have it be tied tightly to one of your joys. That way the work you do to pull it off will not only result in connecting some awesome people, but you will get to share with them your joy.

My tips for finding your signature event are these:

- Brainstorm ideas related to your joys.
- Then float a few of your ideas by some trusted friends.
- Pick one event idea to try out.
- Start small the first time you do your event.
- Evaluate how it went.
- Adjust and try it again.

Committing to myself to do some signature events each year has pushed me.

Networking at Wrigley

As I mentioned, one of my joys is attending Chicago Cubs weekday baseball games at Wrigley Field. The lunch and Cubs games are my main signature event. I call it Networking at Wrigley. Each season I do three or four games depending on my guest list and the Cubs' schedule. I have learned over the years that the games need to be in July, August, or September. When I organized a lunch and game in June, inevitably one of my guests would cancel if the weather looked questionable. You will adjust your event as you learn what works and what doesn't work.

The Annual Boozening

A young friend of mine, Marty, organizes a large Halloween party at a neighborhood bar each year. He's in his late twenties. He started his annual event when he was in college. He calls the event The Annual Boozening. His guests pay a flat fee at the door that covers their drinks. They come in costume. Marty awards six prizes for the costumes. He has music.

He has a list of 150 invitees that he updates each year. Each year some cannot make it, others ask if they can bring someone, and it ends up being about 150 people. He sends a save-the-date out two months in advance, the invite out one month prior to the event, and a reminder two weeks before the event.

When I asked Marty why he hosts this event, he explained to me Halloween is one of the biggest days of the year for young adults. He likes giving his friends a plan for it. Plus, he enjoys bringing people together. He said everyone has someone there to catch up with, and others to meet.

Network and Decorate a Wreath

Another one of my joys is Christmas, and I've organized events around the holiday season. For a number of years, I had a wreath decorating networking event. It was very popular with my friends who were working mothers like me. Working mothers were hard for me to get to come together to network, especially in the evenings. I tried a few events like dinners or cocktail parties that didn't get as predictable attendance as the wreath decorating events did. I think wreath decorating worked because the mothers could bring home a beautiful wreath that their family could enjoy.

Throughout the year, as I meet people and catch up with others, I think about whether they would be a good person to extend an invitation to one of my events. I ask myself if they would enjoy the event. I think about who I could connect them to at my event.

Having signature events each year pushes me to keep doing the work of meeting and getting to know people. It will help you to do the same.

ASK FOR HELP

The fourth set of practices are those related to asking for help, such as these:

- ☐ Set a goal and strategy for achieving it that includes leveraging your network.
- ☐ Clearly articulate what you need help with.
- ☐ Ask someone you know and are "caught up with" for help.
- ☐ Reach out to someone you know but are "not caught up with" for help.
- ☐ Ask someone you don't know at all for help (such as an expert, someone you admire).

The *Ask for Help Practices* have been the hardest for me. When thinking about asking someone for help, I have found I am both

- Concerned someone will say no (I feel rejected), and
- Concerned they will say yes (I worry that they will not do a good job).

There's so much evidence that demonstrates the best leaders have mastered asking for help. One such leader is Jamie Dimon who is the CEO of JPMorgan Chase. Dimon was the CEO when I worked there too. I admired his leadership style from the first moment he addressed us as our new CEO.

When 9/11 happened, he lost a number of friends. At that time, in large companies, the fastest way to get a communication to all employees was voice mail. The next day, he sent an all-employees heartfelt voice message, and again the next day and perhaps a third or fourth day. I don't remember his exact words, but I do remember him acknowledging he was hurting and that he knew we were hurting. Plus, I remember him asking each of us to help by continuing to do our jobs. It was powerful. He is an excellent communicator.

I continue to be a huge fan of his.

He was one of the first American leaders to insist key team members come back into the office during the COVID years. It was not a popular stance at the time. But he knew many of his team members needed to be getting back into the office so they could do their jobs better.

He steadfastly responded to criticism touting that face-to-face work is essential for creativity, for younger workers doing apprenticeships, and for management teams.

Not to be bullied by anyone to give in to what he saw as poor management practices, he acknowledged that his preference for in-person work isn't for everyone, then went on to say those who disagree can look for work elsewhere.

To me, he is a principled leader who is devoted to developing future leaders that can build a great company.

In 2019, I read an article about his seven simple rules to be an effective boss. It included "Trust Your Team." He explains that to develop into a leader, you have to master depending on others, and trust is a huge part of that.

Clearly Articulate What You Need Help With

When I am working with a team that has success, my trust in them increases. It's easy for me to trust a team that is winning! How do I get my team to win? It starts with me being able to clearly communicate what I expect and what success looks like. I need to be an excellent communicator, and that is hard important work.

It's the same exercise when asking someone for help. You start with thinking through what you need help with, then break it down into small discrete asks. This makes it more likely that someone can and will help you.

For example if you need a new job, make these types of requests for help from your network:

Referral: *Let me know if you hear of any job openings such as . . . (explain what type of job you are seeking)*

Introduction: *Could you introduce me to any of your friends who work at . . . (specify a company or industry)*

Opinion: *What do you think of this company (leader or job opportunity)?*

Advice: *I am considering two different types of job searches and want to focus on one. Can I talk through them with you?*

Endorsement: *I just interviewed at your company. Would you put in a good word for me?*

How to Ask for Help

If you struggle with asking for help, start by getting into the habit of asking for clarification when someone says something you don't understand. Adopting this simple practice will give you experience that shows you the benefits that come from speaking up.

One place to practice asking for helping this way is in virtual meetings where participants don't put their cameras on.

I have been observing that in virtual meetings often the person speaking is unaware when others in the meeting do not understand them. When you do not understand someone in a meeting, say (or if it's more appropriate type in the chat) one of these phrases:

- "I do not know what that is."
- "Can you please explain?"
- "Tell me more." or "Say more."
- "I don't know anything about that."
- "I am not familiar with that."

Believe me when I tell you this, others in the meeting will be grateful that you spoke up because chances are many of them also had the same question.

YOUR WAY TO BE

Through my experiences training and coaching business networking for over a decade, I have found when you treat the networking practices like a nonnegotiable part of your day, the practices become habits. They become "your way to be."

Part of what helped me overcome the fear of doing the networking practices regularly was Jia Jiang's Rejection Therapy. If you are feeling like you need a boost to help you make the Be-Social Method your "way to be," I recommend you watch Jia's TED Talk called "What I Learned from 100 Days of Rejection." After learning about and practicing Rejection Therapy, I found the confidence to go for it with daily social interactions that before I would have avoided. I know it can help you too.

When you regularly do the networking practices, you will keep your personal network of support strong. Knowing you have the support of others will give you the confidence to go for it and the ability to handle the ups and downs of work and life more easily.

BE-SOCIAL NETWORKING PRACTICES

Here is a worksheet I give my How Wrigley Field Made Me a Better Networker workshop participants to use to assess their networking practices. I recommend you also assess your practices. For each practice, ask yourself if the practice is something you always do (A), sometimes do (S), or never do (N). Then review your results and consider what you will work on first in order to master the Be-Social Method.

Some practices will seem easy, and others hard. Start with selecting at least one practice for each set to work on consistently doing.

Be-Social Networking Practices Self-Assessment		
For each practice, check how often you do the practice: A for Always, S for Sometimes, N for Never		
1. Meet More People	A	S	N
Introduce yourself to someone you don't know at a party/event or out and about.	□	□	□
Ask people you meet about their work/profession.	□	□	□
Engage with people on social media to meet them (LinkedIn, Facebook, Instagram, X).	□	□	□
Attend larger (more than ten people) networking events put on by others.	□	□	□
Participate in formal organizations (professional, charitable, hobby/special interest, religious, political) or work on a passion project/side gig.	□	□	□
2. Get to Know More People	A	S	N
Exchange "elevator speeches" and stories.	□	□	□

Join an organization (professional, charitable, hobby/special interest, religious, political) and lead a group such as a committee.	☐	☐	☐
Invite someone to network "over coffee" —less than thirty minutes.	☐	☐	☐
Invite someone to network "over lunch/drinks/dinner"—one hour plus.	☐	☐	☐
Engage digitally with someone to get to know them via extended chat or text.	☐	☐	☐
3. Connect People	A	S	N
Introduce people to each other at events/meetings.	☐	☐	☐
Introduce people you know to each other over text or email.	☐	☐	☐
Spend time considering who you should connect and why.	☐	☐	☐
Introduce a small group (two to three others) to each other at an event hosted by you.	☐	☐	☐
Host a large (four or more) event for people to meet or reconnect with others.	☐	☐	☐
4. Ask for Help	A	S	N
Set a goal and strategy for achieving it that includes leveraging your network.	☐	☐	☐
Clearly articulate what you need help with.	☐	☐	☐
Ask someone you know and are "caught up with" for help.	☐	☐	☐
Reach out to someone you know but are "NOT caught up with" for help.	☐	☐	☐
Ask someone you "don't know at all" for help (such as an expert, someone you admire).	☐	☐	☐

Leaders, your team members need to see you model the Be-Social Method. So make the building blocks your own. Start with taking stock in your current network of support and consider your potential network. Take time to really know and appreciate who your people are. Work on your answers to "What do you do for fun?" and "What are you working on?" Ask these questions to some trusted friends and share your answers with them.

Become familiar with the networking practices that are part of the Be-Social Method. Take note of which practices you do always, which ones you do sometimes, and which practices you never do.

Embracing these building blocks will make you a better model for the Be-Social Method, make you a better networker, and, as a bonus, you will start to feel awesome.

Introverts and Extroverts and Those Who Are Both

When pushing your team members to develop their key soft skills, consider asking them if they identify with being an introvert or extrovert. An easy way to do this is to show them the definitions included here:

Introvert

Introverts prefer the inner life of the mind over the outer world of other people. Compared to extroverts, introverts enjoy subdued and solitary experiences.

Extrovert

Extroverts are characterized by outgoingness, high energy, and/or talkativeness. Extroverts recharge, or draw energy, from being with other people compared to introverts who draw energy from being alone.

When you know if a team member is an introvert or an extrovert, you can steer them toward the Be-Social practices that appear to be the best fit.

Here are the practices I recommend introverts master first:

- Meet More People: Ask people you meet about their work/profession.
- Get to Know More People: Exchange "elevator speeches" and stories.
- Connect People: Introduce people to each other at event/meetings.
- Ask for Help: Set a goal and strategy for achieving it that includes leveraging your network.

Tips for Those Who Have Gotten Rusty at Networking Practices

When people were reentering work after the pandemic, clinical psychologist Jennifer Guttman offered tips to help workers reengage their social skills. I have adapted these tips for those adopting the Be-Social Method.

1. **It's okay if it feels forced.** Some of the Be-Social activities may feel robotic at first. If a practice is

something you never do, it will feel awkward at the outset and that is all right. Over time, your muscle memory will kick in, and it will feel easier if you exercise patience.

2. **Model others.** Research shows introverts take their cues from extroverts and then try to push themselves to be extroverted until it feels more natural. Take note when you see someone doing one of the practices you are working on well. I have a friend Margie who is amazing at making introductions. She always includes a sincere compliment about each person. I try to be like Margie when I make introductions.

3. **Schedule downtime.** When pushing yourself to Be-Social, if you are an introvert, be sure to schedule in some downtime. This gives your brain recovery time from social interactions. I like to schedule a quick walk after a meeting that I know is going to be intense or dense with information. The walk (usually to Starbucks!) gives me time to process the meeting.

NINE

KEY SOFT SKILLS

What Happened?

I don't understand what happened to Jennifer, Barbara H. told me. Barbara is a senior VP in healthcare.

Jennifer persistently pursued us for an interview. She was emailing, leaving comments on our social media posts. Day after day, we were hearing from her. This went on for weeks until we scheduled an interview. Which, by the way, she nailed. She came in confident, positive, articulate, and blew me away.

I hired her as an entry-level salesperson. She sailed through the training, impressing her colleagues who were bringing her along on calls.

After her six months of training ended, she seemed ready to sell on her own. We met, and I congratulated her on completing the training. I reviewed her goals with her, and we scheduled our biweekly check-ins.

Then everything changed.

She wasn't doing the work. At least, there was no evidence of it. She wasn't filling out her call information in Salesforce. She did show up for her check-ins with me but didn't have anything to show me or anything to say.

EARLY CAREER EMPLOYEES ARE DIFFERENT THAN BEFORE

Leaders are seeing a significantly large portion of early career employees struggling with the transition into the workplace. Barbara's experience with Jennifer was no exception, but certainly surprising. What's going on?

- 41 percent of business leaders believe Gen Z graduates are unprepared for the workforce.

- 51 percent of Gen Z say their education has not prepared them for the workforce.

Many organizations report Gen Zers lack essential soft skills, with 70 percent of business leaders highlighting poor communication skills.

Before now, there was not much of a need to assess and address a new hire's soft skills in a formal way. Previous early career employees were able to get up the learning curve of the nuanced cultural ways of behaving quickly enough. It seemed to be simply through observation and repeated exposure.

Contributing to the longer learning curve has to be the fact that today many offices have fewer people physically in the offices than before the pandemic. This is compounded when a new hire's direct manager is not in the office at the same time as they are.

When I was talking with my twenty-five-year-old son about this phenomenon, he suggested, "They should get paid differently." When I asked him what he meant by that, he explained he thought people managers who came in the office should get paid more than people managers who did not.

I think it's a good point. When someone's job includes managing and mentoring early career employees and they used to do this before the pandemic, through regular in-person interactions and now they don't, their job has changed. It makes sense to me that their compensation should be evaluated.

On the flip side of that, if leaders are mentoring and developing employees in the office, they should be compensated for this.

EYE ROLLING

Experts studying the phenomena of the dramatic differences in this generation of young adults point to weak in real life (IRL) social skills such as communication that present as a lack of professionalism and can lead to eye rolls by their managers.

Managers of Generation Z workers report their resistance to in-person meetings, expressing verbally dissenting points of view and questioning of someone when they do not understand what they are saying in group meetings.

WHY ARE THEY SO DIFFERENT?

I have learned through my research that this generation had less unsupervised play time than generations before them. Unsupervised time together is when children, teens, and college students learn how to push the limits, deal with fear, solve problems, deal with anger, and get along with peers. Additionally, the youngest generation in the workplace simply has had less time IRL observing others with these skills while they were growing up.

- As children, they played more video games and played less with other children IRL.
- As teens, they entertained themselves on social media and attended fewer parties with peers.
- In college, they stayed connected with old friends digitally and befriended fewer new people.

As a result, when they get to the workplace, they are not showing up with honed real-life social skills. They are more awkward at meeting people in person and hesitant to take the initiative to build relationships with them.

Without these foundational social skills gleaned from practice in life, they are establishing fewer relationships at work. Many are lonely and struggle at work.

WEAKER SOFT SKILLS

When researching and reflecting on this problem, I thought of my own transformation when I embraced business networking. I began (and still do) to treat working on relationship building practices like a nonnegotiable part of my day. I set out to do this work so that I would be better able to navigate the reality that jobs come and go, and I needed to be prepared for the next time I needed a new job.

What I didn't expect was that this effort would result in my having more energy and feeling better. Susan Pinker's book *The Village Effect: How Face-to-Face Contact Can Make Us Healthier and Happier* explains why this happened to me.

MORE FACE-TO-FACE INTERACTIONS

Turns out the work I do to build and maintain my personal network of support strengthens my mental and physical health. Pinker explains its how the human body is wired. She convincingly lays out the research that backs up her assertions.

My key take-aways from her good work are:

- **Social bonds enhance resilience**: When you have a strong network of support, you are more resilient to stress and adversity.

- **In-person communication fosters empathy**: In-person interactions help you develop empathy and understanding toward others.

- **Physical presence boosts mental health**: Regular face-to-face contact can reduce feelings of loneliness and depression.

- **Building social skills**: Engaging in face-to-face interactions helps you develop essential social skills needed for personal and professional success.

- **Enhancing communication skills**: Face-to-face conversations help you improve your verbal and nonverbal communication skills.

- **Creating lasting relationships**: Your in-person interactions are more likely to lead to deep and lasting friendships compared to online interactions.

> Build your Network of Support
> ↓
> Improve your Key Soft Skills & Health

Learning this made me want to get as many Gen Zers as I could to take my networking workshops. They are struggling with loneliness, and I decided they needed the Be-Social Method. I set out to expand my workshops beyond the Career Transition Center in Chicago and make it a digital course that I could market broadly to thousands of Gen Zers.

HOW TO REACH THEM

To figure out how to promote my networking workshop to early career employees, I took Amy Porterfield's Digital Course Academy in hopes that I could figure out how to attract Gen Z to my course. One of the early steps in Porterfield's process is to interview your "Ideal Customer Avatar" to understand what would make the course attractive to them.

What I learned from my interviews with several Gen Zers is that in almost all cases they had no interest in taking a business networking course to work on building their personal network of support.

They very politely explained to me that they didn't see the need to work on networking even if it did improve their soft skills. However, in almost all instances they said they would take the course if their manager asked them to and paid for it.

This information made me pause.

I thought about the young adults who had been coming to my workshops. Before 2017, out of twenty attendees, I would have zero people below the age of thirty. Then in 2017, one, two, and now sometimes three or four Gen Zers are joining the older folks I consistently see. It's so interesting.

Jen Marr, author of *Lifting Up: The Transformative Power of Supportive Leadership* and her first book *Showing Up*, interpreted the disconnect between what the Gen Z interviewees were telling me and the fact that I have some Gen Z workshop attendees.

She said that the young adults who are coming to my course are the type of people who seek self-care. I thought of Alicia, my workshop participant who said to me after spending three hours in my networking workshop, "I don't know how to talk to anyone except my family members."

Marr explained to me that people on the opposite end of the mental health wellness spectrum are those who struggle outwardly with well-being. They need clinical care like therapy, counseling, or hospitalization. Often, someone directs them to get care because of their behavior. In the workplace, it's usually their manager. There are more mental health resources available to employees than ever before, and such access is appreciated by employees.

A recent American Psychological Association Work in America survey highlighted that 77 percent of workers are satisfied with the mental health support they receive from their employers, and 59 percent agree that their employer regularly provides information about available mental health resources.

Marr went on to tell me that most Gen Zers who struggle with loneliness are in the middle group. They don't present behaviors at work that cause a manager to direct them to outside resources. Plus, they lack either the self-awareness of loneliness or the initiative to take action the way my Gen Z workshop participants do.

Marr was not surprised that almost all of the young adults I interviewed said "no thanks" to a skills-building networking course. She explained, "They don't want to be public with their struggle." Instead, they struggle privately, often not opening up to anyone. She continued, "What they need is someone to see them in their struggle and offer them encouragement. This can be friends, family, coworkers, peers, mentors, and leaders."

I thought about what Marr said. It made sense to me. I needed to pivot.

Most of the early career employees that are struggling with their soft skills are the large group in the middle. They are at work. They don't see a reason to work on their soft skills. They told me they are not going to take networking workshops to build their relationship skills. To reach this group that is the largest, I need you, the workplace leader, who wants your team to win.

WARM DEMANDER LEADERS NEEDED

When you see a team member struggling in their job because of poor soft skills, you can help.

Like warm demander teachers whose students trusted them and inspired them to engage and pushed them to excel, when you establish an authentic positive relationship with your team members, they will engage and do the work you ask them to do, even when it's uncomfortable because they trust you.

To do this, you need to roll up your sleeves and coach soft skill development. The Be-Social Method gives you the words to use to do this.

Key Soft Skills

With the Be-Social Method, a set of key soft business skills are named. This is the subset of soft skills that you as a leader can start with, as you purposefully coach soft skills. You tie a key soft skill to a specific practice that you ask your team member to do and that you can observe.

BE-SOCIAL PRACTICES BUILD KEY SOFT SKILLS

KEY SOFT SKILLS

MEET MORE PEOPLE

- Charisma
- Confidence
- Conversational Competence
- Positivity

CONNECT PEOPLE

- Creativity
- Empathy
- Event Planning
- Facilitation

GET TO KNOW MORE PEOPLE

- Curiosity
- Initiative
- Planning and Organization
- Prioritization

ASK FOR HELP

- Care (self, others)
- Humility (strength)
- Trust
- Vulnerability (courage)

BE-SOCIAL PRACTICES

The Be-Social Method is made up of four sets of practices—meeting people, getting to know people, connecting people, and asking for help. When you do these practices routinely, you not only build your personal network, you also develop business skills that make you better at work. These skills are called key soft skills.

Key Soft Skill	Be-Social Networking Practices			
	Meet More People	Get to Know People	Connect People	Ask for Help
Care (self, others)				x
Charisma	x			
Confidence	x			
Conversational Competence	x			
Creativity			x	
Curiosity		x		
Empathy			x	
Event Planning			x	
Facilitation			x	
Humility (strength)				x
Initiative		x		
Planning and Organization		x		
Positivity	x			
Prioritization		x		
Trust				x
Vulnerability (courage)				x

The Be-Social Key Skills Checklist. Use this as a checklist for mastery.

For your team member who is not performing with nuanced parts of their job that require skills listed in the first column of the checklist, highlight which of those skills you think they need to strengthen. Then see if a number of them group under one of the Be-Social Method networking practices.

Key Soft Skill	Be-Social Networking Practices			
	Meet More People	Get to Know People	Connect People	Ask for Help
Care (self, others)				x
Charisma	x			
Confidence	x			
Conversational Competence	x			
Creativity			x	
Curiosity		x		
Empathy			x	
Event Planning			x	
Facilitation			x	
Humility (strength)				x
Initiative		x		
Planning and Organization		x		
Positivity	x			
Prioritization		x		
Trust				x
Vulnerability (courage)				x

The checklist example for James

For example, if you have a team member, James, who needs to work on "positivity and conversational competence," you steer your coaching toward the meet more people practices. For him, you would make a concerted effort to model how to meet more people. You could include James with you when you walk to get coffee and have him witness you greeting people with a "good morning" and striking up conversations with patrons at the coffee shop.

You also consider James's job and assign him the duty to be first person at your weekly team meeting where he is to greet each person, track their attendance, and make small talk with the group until you are ready for the meeting to begin.

I created the key soft skills checklist for you. It's meant to be a guide for you to use when determining your coaching plan for your team member whose performance needs improving because they need to strengthen one or more of their key soft skills.

Think of it as an assessment tool. You are sensing that your team member is struggling, so by using the checklist, you name the skills that need attention. From there you can turn your concerns into action.

Elevator Pitch

Gen Z loves to learn and improve when they are convinced their effort will result in an acceptable yield. As their leader, you can point out to them the importance of a personal network of support and introduce them to the Be-Social Method and Be-Social networking practices.

Here's what you say to your team member:

The Be-Social Method is a framework for creating and maintaining your professional network of support. In business, each of us needs our own personal network of people who support and encourage each other.

Leaders, I know that many of you can tell that Generation Z is struggling at work. Many of them do not reach out for support unless they find a leader they feel they can trust. Generational researchers tell us Gen Z employees are seeking a safe place to work, where their manager is like a coach or parent to them. They really do want to learn and grow on the job. They also want belonging, and when they find it, they will work hard, contribute greatly, and be delighted to stay.

When you push your team members to address their key soft skill gaps, you will find productive and loyal team members. You can see your team members transform from:

- **Invisible to visible**, as they effortlessly meet more people

- **Dull to dynamic**, as they master how to get to know more people

- **Wallflower to connector**, as they bring people they know together

- **Silent sufferer to go-getter**, as they learn how to ask for help

When your team members strengthen their key soft skills, they will be better at working with people. They will be happier and healthier and primed to be your next set of leaders. You will find further enlightenment about these areas in the next and final part of this book.

PART III

I am a lifelong Marquette University men's basketball fan. Since the 2021–2022 season, I have had so much fun following the current coach Shaka Smart.

I was watching a game his first season when I heard the announcer talk about a metric Shaka tracks at games and practices called EGBs. "EGBs" are Energy Generating Behaviors.

According to the Marquette basketball glossary, an EGB is any action that creates energy and positively affects those around us. EGBs increase readiness and aggressiveness, they build momentum after positive plays, and they stem the tide during challenging stretches. Examples include floor slaps, daps, first to the floors, encouragement, acknowledgments, power claps, and chest bumps.

I love EGBs as a metric. I wish every leader defined EGBs for their team and tracked them.

Beyond EGBs, Coach Smart analyzes his individual players' performance and tailors practice sessions to address their specific needs. He ensures each team member gets the opportunity and push needed to grow.

Smart is a warm demander leader. He encourages relationship building so much he measures it. Plus, he demonstrates his commitment to each team member's personal growth by pushing them with specific improvement goals that he measures. His Marquette players not only develop their athletic abilities but also grow as individuals, learning the value of teamwork, resilience, and dedication.

Shaka Smart is the type of leader I wish every young adult had.

PERSONALIZED COACHING USING THE BE-SOCIAL METHOD

As a leader, you most likely have a method for coaching your team members. In Part III here, I offer you a framework called the Five-Step Approach to use for coaching your team members on the key soft skills they need for relationship building in the workplace. It is meant to be illustrative and complement what you already do and inspire you to start coaching key soft skills development.

The following four chapters provide examples of the Five-Step Approach.

FIVE-STEP APPROACH

① CHECKLIST

Fill out **Be-Social Key Soft Skills checkist** for your team member.

Determine which set of **Be-Social networking practices** your team member needs to work on.

② ROLE MODEL

Be an **Obvious Role Model** of the practices you want your team member to work on.

③ TRIAL BALLOON

Select **one behavior or task** for your team member to demonstrate over the next few weeks.

④ ASSESSMENT

Align with your team member on a **set of Be-Social networking practices** to assess and address together that will further their growth.

⑤ ACTION PLAN

Meet regularly to **review progress** on new behaviors and/or practices.

CELEBRATE VICTORIES ALL ALONG THE WAY

135

As a warm demander leader, you will have built good relationships with your team members. As a result, your team members will trust and respect you and will be open to the coaching that you provide them.

START HERE

When you can see a team member is struggling with the part of their job that involves soft skills, follow the Five-Step Approach to push them to grow and win. Begin your coaching preparation of soft skills by using the Be-Social Key Skills Checklist, introduced in the previous chapter.

The checklist for your team member shows the Be-Social networking practices (meet people, get to know people, connect people, ask for help) that develop the key soft skills.

STEP 1: Checklist

Find and highlight the skills you believe your team member needs to strengthen using the Be-Social Key Skills Checklist. Then see which set of the Be-Social Method networking practices (meet people, get to know people, connect people, ask for help) they need to work on.

STEPS 2 through 5: Role Model, Trial Balloon, Assessment, Action Plan

Armed with this information from the checklist, you can design a personalized coaching plan for your team member following

Steps 2 through 5 to address the soft skill development they need. It begins with you making a conscious effort to model the skills you are promoting while confirming if your team member is up for the task of developing the skills. After which, you put an action plan together.

WORKSHEETS AND AI

I reference some worksheets in the following chapters to assist you with your coaching, which you can find in the Appendix. The *Exercises and Resources* worksheet is for you to give to your team member. In it, you will see I include AI Companion prompts for them to use to find related videos and articles.

Since November 2023, I have been using AI Companion tools such as Copilot and ChatGPT to assist me just about every day. I recommend you do the same so you become familiar with this technology that is in the workplace and here to stay.

I have found using AI Companion to be a big time saver. It's like I have a junior team member available to help me. What's also been interesting for me is that by using the AI Companion, I have learned through trial and error to be more specific in my instruction.

Which coincidently is also what Gen Z needs from their leaders. Many of them take instructions quite literally just like the AI Companion does. This is because these young adults are not as good at picking up nuance in language. I know that with more and more workplace experiences, they will get better at this essential communication skill. In the meantime, like a good change leader, meet them where they are. Provide as specific instructions as you can.

The following four chapters provide examples of how a leader such as you would address a team member struggling with soft skills using the Five-Step Approach.

- Chapter 10 Invisible to Visible addresses a team member who needs to work on the *Meet More People Practices*.

- Chapter 11 Dull to Dynamic addresses a team member who needs to work on the *Get to Know More People Practices*.

- Chapter 12 Wallflower to Purposeful Collaborator addresses a team member who needs to work on the *Connect People Practices*.

- Chapter 13 Silent Sufferer to Go-Getter addresses a team member who needs to work on the *Ask for Help Practices*.

Use the following table as a way to differentiate among key soft skills. The graphic provides a definition and examples of strong performance and weak performance.

To recap, the Five-Step Approach is a guide. It is meant to get you started on coaching soft skill development. Trust your experience as a leader when assessing your team members' soft skills and determining which practices would help them strengthen the soft skills they need to perform their job better.

Key Soft Skill	Definition	Examples of Strong Performance	Examples of Weak Performance
Care (self, others)	Showing concern for oneself and others' well-being	- Gets needed physical and mental care - Offers help - Encourages others	- Ignores own needs - Overlooks others' struggles - Avoids support
Charisma	Attracting and inspiring others through personality and charm	- Engages team - Motivates peers - Builds rapport	- Fails to engage - Lacks enthusiasm - Struggles to connect
Confidence	Believing in oneself and one's abilities	- Takes on challenges - Speaks up in meetings - Makes decisions	- Hesitates to act - Avoids speaking - Shies away from tasks
Conversational Competence	Effectively engaging in and managing conversations	- Maintains eye contact - Responds appropriately - Keeps discussions on track	- Gives irrelevant responses - Loses focus - Shows disinterest
Creativity	Generating new and innovative ideas	- Proposes unique solutions - Thinks outside the box - Improves processes	- Sticks to routine - Avoids new ideas - Lacks innovation
Curiosity	Eager to learn and explore new things	- Asks questions - Researches topics - Seeks feedback	- Sticks to known methods - Ignores feedback - Shows disinterest

Key Soft Skill	Definition	Examples of Strong Performance	Examples of Weak Performance
Empathy	Understanding and sharing the feelings of others	- Listens actively - Supports colleagues - Acknowledges feelings	- Dismisses emotions - Shows insensitivity - Lacks understanding
Event Planning	Organizing and managing events effectively	- Coordinates resources - Communicates plans - Manages timelines	- Misses deadlines - Poor coordination - Fails to communicate
Facilitation	Guiding groups to achieve goals and outcomes	- Leads meetings - Encourages participation - Keeps focus	- Fails to resolve conflicts - Loses focus - Dominates discussions
Humility (strength)	Recognizing one's limitations and valuing others' contributions	- Seeks advice - Credits team - Admits mistakes	- Avoids advice - Denies errors - Takes all credit
Initiative	Taking action without being prompted	- Starts projects - Solves problems - Volunteers for tasks	- Waits for instructions - Avoids responsibility - Lacks motivation
Planning and Organization	Arranging tasks and resources efficiently	- Sets priorities - Meets deadlines - Manages resources	- Misses deadlines - Poor time management - Disorganized

Key Soft Skill	Definition	Examples of Strong Performance	Examples of Weak Performance
Positivity	Maintaining a positive attitude and outlook	- Encourages team - Handles stress well - Celebrates successes	- Easily stressed - Overlooks achievements - Pessimistic
Prioritization	Determining the order of tasks based on importance	- Identifies key tasks - Focuses on goals - Adjusts priorities	- Misjudges task importance - Easily distracted - Fails to adjust
Trust	Building and maintaining reliable relationships	- Keeps promises - Communicates openly - Respects confidentiality	- Breaks promises - Withholds information - Breaches confidentiality
Vulnerability (courage)	Willingness to show one's true self and take risks	- Shares ideas - Seeks feedback - Takes risks	- Hides mistakes - Avoids feedback - Fears risks

The Be-Social Method Key Soft Skills definitions and examples

TEN

INVISIBLE TO VISIBLE

A manager related this story to me:

Always on Mute

Michael is the youngest member of our operations team. He was brought in as an operations engineer to help us write up our business requirements for a new system, then help us evaluate the best solution and get it in place.

This is his first professional job. He is sharp, fresh out of business school. He went to business school directly after getting his industrial engineering degree.

He was friendly enough when I introduced him to the team, but after two months he has yet to utter a word in our meetings. He prefers to take the meetings from his desk with his camera off, rather than join us in the conference room.

After the meeting, he and I will debrief, and it's clear to me that he understands what's going on in the meeting. So that's not the issue.

The other day, when I asked him about a tough meeting we had just had, he offered a great point that I wish he had shared in the meeting. If he had, we could have avoided going in the wrong direction during that meeting.

I told him as much and when I did, his face turned red with embarrassment.

I am at a loss with how to help him be more visible in meetings.

SITUATION TO IMPROVE: THE INVISIBLE TEAM MEMBER

Let's say Michael is your team member. Michael is rarely engaging in person with others at work. Michael seems invisible. You have observed that he does not initiate verbal conversation. He prefers to stay at his desk and join meetings virtually rather than joining others in a conference room.

On virtual calls, Michael joins the call with his camera off and his mute button on. When someone directly asks him a question, he turns off his mute button and answers; otherwise, he does not engage. This behavior is holding Michael and your team back.

USE THE FIVE-STEP APPROACH

You decide to coach Michael using the Five-Step Approach.

STEP 1: Checklist

You review the *Be-Social Key Skills Checklist* and highlight skills you need Michael to strengthen. This shows you Michael needs to work on the meet more people practices.

Key Soft Skill	Be-Social Networking Practices			
	Meet More People	Get to Know People	Connect People	Ask for Help
Care (self, others)				x
Charisma	x			
Confidence	x			
Conversational Competence	x			
Creativity			x	
Curiosity		x		
Empathy			x	
Event Planning			x	
Facilitation			x	
Humility (strength)				x
Initiative		x		
Planning and Organization		x		
Positivity	x			
Prioritization		x		
Trust				x
Vulnerability (courage)				x

Example for Michael who needs to work on his *Meet More People* skills

145

STEP 2: Role Model

You become an obvious role model of the practices you want Michael to work on. You demonstrate your interest in meeting people by doing these practices and others:

- You always attend meetings in person when in the same building as the meeting, and when you must attend virtual meetings, you always have your camera on.

- When someone new joins your in-person or virtual meeting, you introduce yourself and others to them.

STEP 3: Trial Balloon

You consider what your trial balloon should be for Michael. A *trial balloon* is a test done to gauge results before making a final decision. In this case, you will be gauging Michael's ability to work on the *Meet More People Practices*. You ask Michael to do the following:

- Make an effort to attend meetings in person when in the same building as the meeting.

- Make an effort to consistently join both in-person or virtual meetings early and to greet each person by name before the meeting starts.

STEP 4: Assessment

After a few weeks, you evaluate how well Michael has been doing with this trial balloon test.

You determine he has been doing well and that you believe Michael can grow further. You set up a coaching meeting with him. At it, you have a conversation with him about how you have observed he's been attending more meetings in person and showing up for meetings early and greeting people.

You express your desire to see him grow his soft skills. (If the trial balloon did not go well, partner with your manager or human resources business partner to discuss other options to try.)

You introduce Michael to the Be-Social Method networking practices (refer to chapter 8). You give him the *Meet More People Self-Assessment* (refer to the worksheet in the Appendix) and ask him to complete it and then schedule some time to meet with you to review it.

When you meet with Michael to review his responses, you cover the points in your *Leader Guide: Meet More People Self-Assessment Review* (see Appendix).

STEP 5: Action Plan

During the meeting, when you ask Michael if the practices listed in *Meet More People Self-Assessment* seemed easy or hard, he tells you he thinks they are hard. You look over the related key soft skills together. You ask him which of these skills he thinks he needs to strengthen.

He says conversational competence is something he wants to work on. You give Michael the *Meet More People Exercises and Resources* (see Appendix). He finds conversational competence on the list and agrees to do the elevator exercise. You determine when and how you will check in with Michael on progress.

Leaders, do you have a team member who does not introduce themselves to others in meetings or at work events or a team member who is always one of the last to join the meeting and one of the first to leave a meeting? If so, push them to work on *Meet More People Practices.*

Then watch your team member transform from someone who only speaks in meetings when they have been asked a direct question to someone who shows up early to meetings to greet everyone and is even quick to introduce a new person to the group.

ELEVEN

DULL TO DYNAMIC

An HR manager told me this story:

Nothing Extra

Emma has been on my team for over a year. She shows up and gets her work done. Her work is sufficient, but she never delivers anything extra. People on our team know her and value her work but don't expect anything exceptional to come from her. They have stopped seeking her out for counsel. She has declined their invitations to provide support so often. She seems uninterested in what they are working on and frankly in getting to know any of them personally.

I don't think she has one person on the team that she would call her friend. This is holding her back. She has not built the type of relationships with others on our team that afford her the opportunity to see how she can go above and beyond and provide extra value.

SITUATION TO IMPROVE: DULL TEAM MEMBER

Emma is your team member. She does exactly what you ask her to do and then stops. She doesn't take the initiative to provide extra value or pitch in to help others. She doesn't seem to have formed relationships with others on the team beyond the basics: name and job title.

Since she has been in her role for more than a year, you expected her to have formed relationships with team members resulting in synergies that can create some big wins for your team. You have not seen the growth in her soft skills that you expected. She's become the weak link in your team.

You decide to coach Emma using the Five-Step Approach.

STEP 1: Checklist

You review the *Be-Social Key Skills Checklist* and highlight the skills you need Emma to strengthen. This shows you Emma needs to work on the *Get to Know More People Practices*.

Key Soft Skill	Be-Social Networking Practices			
	Meet More People	Get to Know People	Connect People	Ask for Help
Care (self, others)				x
Charisma	x			
Confidence	x			
Conversational Competence	x			
Creativity			x	
Curiosity		x		
Empathy			x	
Event Planning			x	
Facilitation			x	
Humility (strength)				x
Initiative		x		
Planning and Organization		x		
Positivity	x			
Prioritization		x		
Trust				x
Vulnerability (courage)				x

Example for Emma who needs to work on her
***Get to Know More People* skills**

STEP 2: Role Model

You become an obvious role model for the practices you want Emma to work on. You demonstrate interest in getting to know more people by doing this practice and others:

- At your weekly staff meeting, you designate the first ten minutes as a photo share. Each week you assign one team member to bring a personal photograph to share with the team and explain what it is and why they chose it to share. You ask questions and encourage others to join in the discussion to get to know more about the team member sharing the photograph and also, in doing so, offer information about themselves.

STEP 3: Trial Balloon

You consider what your trial balloon should be for Emma. A *trial balloon* is a test done to gauge results before making a final decision. In this case, you will be gauging Emma's ability to work on the *Get to Know More People Practices.*

You ask Emma to interview one of your team members to learn about their new project as well as some fun facts about them. First she is to draft an interview guide for your review. Then you will establish a deadline for her to turn in a summary to present at a future staff meeting.

STEP 4: Assessment

After Emma has completed her trial balloon task, you evaluate how it went. You determine it went well and that you believe Emma can grow further. You set up a coaching meeting with her. At it, you have a conversation with her about her positive performance with interviewing her team member and presenting the summary to her team, and your desire to see her grow her soft skills. (If it did not go well, partner with your manager or human resources business partner to discuss other options to try.)

You introduce her to the Be-Social Method networking practices (refer to chapter 8). You give Emma the *Get to Know More People Self-Assessment* (see Appendix) and ask her to complete it and then schedule some time to meet with you to review it. When you meet with her to review her responses, you cover the points in your *Leader Guide: Get to Know More People Self-Assessment Review* (see Appendix).

STEP 5: Action Plan

During the meeting, when you ask Emma if the practices listed in the *Get to Know More People Self-Assessment* seemed easy or hard. She tells you she thinks they are hard. You look over the related key soft skills together. You ask her which of these skills she thinks she needs to strengthen. She says the planning and organization skill is something she wants to work on.

You give her the *Get to Know More People Exercises and Resources* (see Appendix). She finds planning and organization and agrees to do the Daily Achiever Skills Exercise. You determine when and how you will check in on progress with Emma.

Leaders, do you have a team member who holds back on engaging with the team or a team member that does not seem to even be aware of what others on your team do? If so, push them to work on *Get to Know More People Practices*.

Then watch your team member transform from someone who does the minimum required when it comes to their job and getting to know their team members to someone who is curious about others and takes the initiative to go the extra mile for the team.

TWELVE

WALLFLOWER TO PURPOSEFUL COLLABORATOR

Here is the story of an employee from a midlevel manager:

Hangs Back

Hannah shows up to every company function. She comes to all our client mixers too. While her dedication is impressive, I have noticed she only talks one-on-one with people, and the only people she talks with are those she already knows.

Plus, in our team meetings she never jumps into the middle of a conversation to contribute. Based on my observations I question if she is ready for the next level of responsibility. It includes running meetings and hosting events. I am not sure she's got the skills needed to drive collaboration in our environment.

SITUATION TO IMPROVE: WALLFLOWER TEAM MEMBER

Your team member Hannah has not demonstrated an ability to bring people together to collaborate. Given the choice, instead of pulling together team members to address an opportunity or problem, she opts to work on it by herself and present her idea to you alone. When she is put in a group to work on an issue, Hannah will engage but it's limited to her offering her point of view. Plus, you have noticed she bristles when her ideas are challenged. Her behavior is limiting her capacity to grow.

STEP 1: Checklist

You review the *Be-Social Key Soft Skills Checklist* and highlight the skills you need Hannah to strengthen. This shows you Hannah needs to work on the *Connect People Practices*.

Key Soft Skill	Be-Social Networking Practices			
	Meet More People	Get to Know People	Connect People	Ask for Help
Care (self, others)				x
Charisma	x			
Confidence	x			
Conversational Competence	x			
Creativity			x	
Curiosity		x		
Empathy			x	
Event Planning			x	
Facilitation			x	
Humility (strength)				x
Initiative		x		
Planning and Organization		x		
Positivity	x			
Prioritization		x		
Trust				x
Vulnerability (courage)			x	

Example for Hannah who needs to work on her *Connect People* skills

STEP 2: Role Model

You become an obvious role model of the practices you want Hannah to work on. You demonstrate interest in connecting people by doing this practice and others:

- You set up and run a series of weekly lunch and learn meetings where you invite a leader from another department and two or three of their team members to discuss with your team the biggest challenge they are facing. You have time before and after the discussion for informal networking.

STEP 3: Trial Balloon

You consider what your trial balloon should be for Hannah. A *trial balloon* is a test done to gauge results before making a final decision. In this case, you will be gauging Hannah's ability to work on the *Connect People Practices.*

You ask Hannah to do the following: Partner with you on facilitating the lunch and learns. During the session, she is to ask the presenters how your team can help them with the challenge they are presenting, then to recap the answers and email them to your team.

STEP 4: Assessment

After Hannah has partnered with you on three of the lunch and learns, you evaluate how your trial balloon went. You determine it went well and that you believe Hannah can grow further. You set up a coaching meeting with her. At it, you have a conversation with her about her positive performance with the lunch and learns and your desire to see her grow her soft skills. (If it did not go well, partner with your manager or human resources business partner to discuss other options to try.)

You introduce her to the Be-Social Method networking practices (refer to chapter 8). You give Hannah the *Connect People Self-Assessment* (see Appendix) and ask her to complete it and then schedule some time to meet with you to review it. When you meet with her to review her responses, you cover the points in your *Leader Guide: Connect People Self-Assessment Review* (see Appendix).

STEP 5: Action Plan

During the meeting, when you ask Hannah if the practices listed in the *Connect People Self-Assessment* seemed easy or hard. She tells you she thinks they are hard. You look over the related key soft skills together. You ask her which of these skills she thinks she needs to strengthen. She says the facilitation skill is something she wants to work on.

You give her the *Connect People Exercises and Resources*. She finds facilitation and agrees to read *10 Tips for Effective Small Group Facilitation* from Global Learning Partners and pick a few of the tips and work on them in everyday conversation. You determine when and how you will check in on progress with Hannah.

Leaders, do you have a team member who avoids bringing people together to collaborate and holds back their ideas in group meetings? If so, push them to work on *Connect People Practices*.

Then watch your team member transform from someone who only produces solo work to someone who can deliver solutions created by bringing together team members to work on your company's toughest problems.

THIRTEEN

SILENT SUFFERER TO GO-GETTER

Jacob was a top recruit for the company. His manager told me this:

Late and Lackluster

Jacob's grades from a prestigious business school were head and shoulders above all others. I was delighted when he accepted our offer and moved across the country to join our team. Yet, since his first day three months ago, I have yet to see evidence of his exceptionalism.

It's not that he isn't putting in the hours. He's always in the office before me and often when I check my Teams app after hours, he is online.

He often seems tired and stressed out, but when I ask him how it's going, he says he's doing fine. His work product is often late. Plus, it lacks the wow factor. I suspect he is not taking advantage of the resources of his teammates when he's putting together his proposals even though I have suggested this a number of times.

SITUATION TO IMPROVE: SILENT SUFFERER

Your team member Jacob struggles delivering his work on time. You have offered assistance. He has yet to take you up on it. He seems uncomfortable showing you work that's not "ready." Lately, he has been showing up at meetings unprepared. You don't think Jacob is lazy, but you wonder if he's procrastinating or striving to deliver work that's too perfect.

You suspect Jacob may be suffering silently and is unable to ask for help, due to pride, embarrassment, or fear of ridicule. This behavior is an issue and causing Jacob to miss deadlines and deliver work that does not have the benefit of others' input.

STEP 1: Checklist

You review the *Be-Social Key Soft Skill Checklist* and highlight the skills you need Jacob to strengthen. This shows you Jacob needs to work on the *Ask for Help Practices*.

Key Soft Skill	Be-Social Networking Practices			
	Meet More People	Get to Know People	Connect People	Ask for Help
Care (self, others)				x
Charisma	x			
Confidence	x			
Conversational Competence	x			
Creativity			x	
Curiosity		x		
Empathy			x	
Event Planning			x	
Facilitation			x	
Humility (strength)				x
Initiative		x		
Planning and Organization		x		
Positivity	x			
Prioritization		x		
Trust				x
Vulnerability (courage)				x

Example for Jacob who needs to work on his *Ask for Help* skills

STEP 2: Role Model

You become an obvious role model of the practices you want Jacob to work on. You demonstrate your comfort in asking for help by doing this practice and others:

- You put a topic on your team meeting agenda each week that you need help understanding. At your meeting, you ask your team members what they know about the topic and for their advice on how to get help learning more about the topic.

STEP 3: Trial Balloon

You consider what your trial balloon should be for Jacob. A trial balloon is a test done to gauge results before making a final decision. In this case, you will be gauging Jacob's ability to work on the *Ask for Help Practices*.

You ask Jacob to do the following: Take your team's latest proposal to three stakeholders and ask them for their feedback on it. You coach him not to defend the proposal but simply to collect their positive and negative feedback, plus their suggestions for how to improve it.

STEP 4: Assessment

After Jacob has completed his trial balloon task, you evaluate how it went. You determine Jacob did a good job with reviewing the team's proposal with stakeholders and that you believe Jacob can grow further.

You set up a coaching meeting with him. At it, you have a conversation with him about his positive performance with the proposal review and your desire to see him grow his soft skills. (If it did not go well, partner with your manager or human resources business partner to discuss other options to try.)

You introduce him to the Be-Social Method networking practices (refer to chapter 8). You give Jacob the *Ask for Help Self-Assessment* (see Appendix) and ask him to complete it and then schedule some time to meet with you to review it.

When you meet with him to review his responses, you cover the points in your *Leader Guide: Ask for Help Self-Assessment Review* (see Appendix).

STEP 5: Action Plan

During the meeting, you ask Jacob if the practices listed in *Ask for Help Self-Assessment* seemed easy or hard. He tells you he thinks they are hard. You look over the related key soft skills together. You ask him which of these skills he thinks he needs to strengthen. He says the vulnerability skill is something he wants to work on.

You give him the *Ask for Help Exercises and Resources* (see Appendix). He finds vulnerability and selects the Skills Exercise: Five-Day Rejection Challenge that will require him to practice being vulnerable.

You determine when and how you will check in on progress with Jacob.

Leaders, do you have a team member who suffers in silence when stumped and rejects your offers of assistance or spends too much time on assignments? If so, push them to work on *Ask for Help Practices*.

Then watch your team member transform from someone who suffers with their work to someone who is constantly leveraging the in-house expertise of their team members to deliver better work, plus getting deeper in their knowledge of your business.

Help People Win by Starting Small

I think a big part of progress is small wins.

For example one of the warm demander requests I've given a lot of people who are struggling with starting to exercise is to do a five-minute stair workout every day.

Most people have access to some stairs.

If someone says they can't do this, I say to them, "There's a bigger problem. Either you don't want to exercise or you choose not to. It's not true that you are too busy to do a five-minute stair exercise."

And when someone says I can do this, then they do it and it does get their heart rate up a bit, it also has the impact of being a victory.

Before they know it, the five minutes on the stairs can be seven minutes and so on.

As warm demanders we can help people win by starting off with something small.

David Rust
President, Coaching Solutions

HOW YOU CAN HELP

I set out to determine how leaders can help Gen Z team members in the workplace that are performing poorly due to struggles with loneliness.

Too many young adults are struggling with loneliness and related mental health issues. These problems are hitting their organization's bottom line due to higher healthcare costs, increased absenteeism, lower productivity, and higher turnover.

In my quest for the right counsel to give leaders, I learned about the teacher style coined *warm demander* by Judith Kleinfeld. Warm demander was how Kleinfeld described teachers who provide personal warmth with high expectations. These teachers insist on high performance while providing a supportive and structured environment.

Gen Z workers struggle with many of the same things the students in the Kleinfeld study and subsequent studies struggled with, including motivation, feeling valued, cultural challenges, and adapting to new environments and new expectations.

Gen Z workers need leaders who insist on high-performance while providing a supportive and structured workplace. Leaders like this, leaders who exhibit warm demander qualities, are everywhere. I interviewed several of these leaders when doing the research for this book.

These warm demander leaders know how to build relationships with their team members and push them to win.

They can model relationship building at work and push their team members who are struggling to work on the Be-Social Method networking practices I've included in this book. When their team members consistently do the practices, they will become more secure, and their performance will improve.

The loneliness and mental health crisis facing our youngest workers is real.

Those struggling in the workplace need leaders who will push them to do the work to transform from feeling lonely to feeling secure.

They need warm demander leaders.

They need you.

ACKNOWLEDGMENTS

Thank you to my husband, John, whom I abandoned several Saturdays so I could do the research and writing that has become this book. I am grateful for your constant support of my work, and I can't wait to enjoy more Florida bike rides with you.

Thank you to my son Daniel, whose insight into popular culture's influence on his generation is only surpassed by his kind heart and ability to get me to laugh. Thank you to my son Chris, whose willingness to join me in absolutely any conversation is a gift that I treasure almost as much as how quickly he says yes to getting together with me or anyone in his large circle of people he cares about.

Thank you to "my people," those of you in my network of support. Your willingness to get together and have meaningful conversations keeps me going, and your willingness to meet other people I send your way reminds me how awesome most people are. My hope is that you can continue to inspire every young person in your life to do that hard work of building and maintaining relationships through your example.

Thank you to Jia Jiang whose Rejection Therapy should be required training for every human. Your and Tracy Xia's openness to my ideas and participation in your Art of Achieving Ambitious Things research was an experience I treasure.

Thank you to Jen Marr who continues to inspire me to keep trying to do what I can to help leaders in the workplace make bigger leaps forward when it comes to their employees' well-being.

Thank you to David Stahl for always having your door open to me and so many others. Your Warm Demander stories provided me with the shorthand "set up forums and let them run" that I know will help leaders see that being 'demanding' is how you push your team to improve, grow and win.

Thank you to Anne Meyer for inspiring the Send Twelve Angel Empathy exercise when you shared your daily prayer ritual with me, years ago when we were eating angel Christmas cookies at Finley Dunne's before the St. Andrew All School Christmas concert.

Thank you to the workplace leaders who have shared stories of frustration with me. Your examples were tremendously helpful. I have kept your identities confidential per your requests. Thanks to those who accepted my request for an interview to hear your warm demander stories. I reached out to you specifically for a reason—it's because you impress me! I thought you would have good stories to help me work through how to make the case for warm demander leaders and you did. I wish I could have put all your stories in this book. My editor, Sandra Wendel, will tell you that I tried to!

You are awesome: Manny Cossi, Patricia Grant, Bob Greco, Barb Hoban, Lori Igleski, Eric Koester, Andy Kotecki, Jim Langhenry, Marty Langhenry, Kevin Long, Jen Marr, Kelly Rice, Kimberly Roessler, David Rust, Charles Shrum and David Stahl. Thank you to the many Gen Zers who accepted my request for an interview. Your input provided me valuable direction for this book. I look forward to staying in touch. Thank you to my anonymous beta readers. Your feedback helped me tremendously. Feedback really is a gift. Thank you, Janica Smith, my publishing navigator and all the wonderful people you found to turn the manuscript into this book, especially my editor Sandra Wendel. Well done!

Thank you, Tom Kelly for recommending the book title – it fits so perfectly. Thank you, Eileen Speidel, for not only reading my manuscript but for reading every blog I write. I sleep better knowing you have given my content your seal of approval. Thank you, Sheila Long for the articles you send me and your constant support. Thank you to my mother, Mary Louise Hildebrandt, the first warm demander in my life. Every day, I am reminded how blessed I am to have you as my mother.

Thank you, Anita Jenke for giving my business networking workshop a home at the Career Transition Center in Chicago. Thank you, Jim Steuer of Think Heart Strategy for getting me to start my newsletter and pushing me to work on my confidence. I learned so much from you.

Thank you to the loyal readers of my newsletter. Please know your replies to me over this past year have given me the energy I've needed to get this book done. I am blessed to have people like you offering me advice and encouraging me.

Let's continue to work together to help every young person we know build their network of support that will help them to find love and joy in their life and success in the workplace.

APPENDIX

This Appendix contains worksheets referenced in Part III.

You can find downloadable PDF versions of these worksheets at www.colleenmcfarland.us.

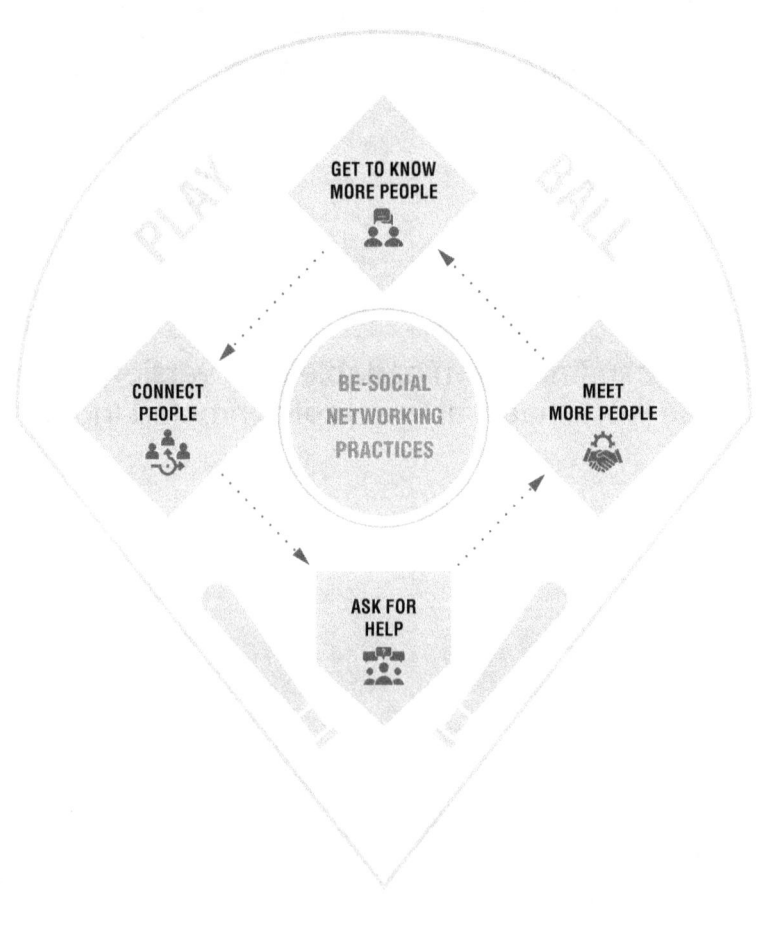

BE-SOCIAL KEY SKILLS CHECKLIST

Key Soft Skill	Be-Social Networking Practices			
	Meet People	Get to Know People	Connect People	Ask for Help
Care (self, others)				x
Charisma	x			
Confidence	x			
Conversational Competence	x			
Creativity			x	
Curiosity		x		
Empathy			x	
Event Planning			x	
Facilitation			x	
Humility (strength)				x
Initiative		x		
Planning and Organization		x		
Positivity	x			
Prioritization		x		
Trust				x
Vulnerability (courage)				x

175

——THE BE-SOCIAL METHOD ——

MEET MORE PEOPLE • SELF-ASSESSMENT

Building Blocks:

What are your joys?

What are you working on?

Which people are your path (and easy to meet)?

Who would you like to meet (that is not your path and requires a plan for you to meet)?

Meet More People Practices:

#1 - Introduce yourself to someone you don't know at a party/event or out and about.

- How often do you do this practice?
  Circle answer: Always, Sometimes, Never

- What activities do you currently do that would give you the opportunity to work on this practice?

_____

_____

- How could you tie working on this practice to one of your joys?

_____

_____

#2 - Ask people you meet about their work/profession.

- How often do you do this practice?
  Circle answer: Always, Sometimes, Never

- What activities do you currently do that would give you the opportunity to work on this practice?

_____

_____

- How could you tie working on this practice to one of your joys?

#3 - Engage with people on social media to meet them (LinkedIn, Facebook, Instagram, X).

- How often do you do this practice?
  Circle answer: Always, Sometimes, Never
- What activities do you currently do that would give you the opportunity to work on this practice?

- How could you tie working on this practice to one of your joys?

#4 - Attend larger (more than ten people) networking events put on by others.

- How often do you do this practice?
  Circle answer: Always, Sometimes, Never

- What activities do you currently do that would give you the opportunity to work on this practice?

_____

_____

_____

- How could you tie working on this practice to one of your joys?

_____

_____

_____

#5 - Participate in formal organizations (professional, charitable, hobby/special interest, religious, political) or work on a passion project/side gig.

- How often do you do this practice?
  Circle answer: Always, Sometimes, Never

- What activities do you currently do that would give you the opportunity to work on this practice?

_____

_____

- How could you tie working on this practice to one of your joys?

_____

_____

HOW TO PUT THIS INTO ACTION

Review the following five *Meet More People Practices*. Decide which practice you will focus on. The practice you pick can be one that you think is easier than the others or a practice that you want to push yourself to try. Tell a trusted friend your plan and make it happen!

Meet More People Practices (pick one to focus on):

- ☐ Introduce yourself to someone you don't know at a party/event or out and about.

- ☐ Ask people you meet about their work/profession.

- ☐ Engage with people on social media to meet them (LinkedIn, Facebook, Instagram, X).

- ☐ Attend larger (more than ten people) networking events put on by others.

- ☐ Participate in a formal organization or work on a passion project/side gig.

——THE BE-SOCIAL METHOD ——

MEET MORE PEOPLE • LEADER GUIDE

Discuss with your team member the following points:

- In business, we are always looking to meet more people who we can potentially work with and partner with to innovate and solve problems.

- In our personal lives, we can and should work on these practices while doing things we are already doing.

- Bonus: Doing the *Meet More People Practices* regularly results in the strengthening of these key soft skills:
  - Conversational Competence
  - Confidence
  - Positivity
  - Charisma

Ask your team member to review their *Meet More People Self-Assessment* responses.

Afterward, ask your team member if the set of practices seems EASY or HARD to them.

- If your team member answers EASY, look at the practices assessed as *Sometimes* or *Never*. Discuss which of these practices they can work on doing *Always*.
  - Note here ideas for doing the practices at work.

- Note here at least one way the team member will do the practices through their joys.

- If your team member answers HARD, look over the list of related key soft skills.
  - Check which of these skills they feel weak in.
    - ☐ Conversational Competence
    - ☐ Confidence
    - ☐ Positivity
    - ☐ Charisma
- Provide them the *Meet More People Exercises and Resources* and discuss. Note here at least one of the exercises they plan to try or resources they plan to reference.

The Be-Social Method
Meet More People
Exercises and Resources

Key Soft Skill: Conversational Competence

☐ **Exercise: Little Cutie**
Give a friendly greeting with a compliment to a stranger: "You have a little cutie there" or "Your dog is so cute."

☐ **Exercise: Checkout Lane**
At the grocery store, engage with someone in a person lane (skip the self-checkout lane). Ask them about something they are buying.

☐ **Exercise: Go Early**
Be first at your in-person or virtual meeting or event and start up a friendly conversation with the next person who arrives. Have an icebreaker ready such as something personal about you and a question for them (for example, ask them what they did over the weekend or if they have a vacation planned).

☐ **Exercise: Elevator**
When you find yourself in an elevator with just one other person, be friendly. Have a smile on your face and make eye contact. Say hello and make small talk with an easy, light comment (weather, TGIF) and leave with a friendly closing ("Have a nice day."). Goal: Get someone to feel your warmth.

☐ **Book:**
Get to What Matters: Tools to Transform Conversations at Work
by Wendy D. Lynch and Clydette de Groot

☐ **Book:**
We Need to Talk: How to Have Conversations That Matter
by Celeste Headlee

☐ **AI Companion prompts:**
I am working on Conversational Competence in a business setting and am looking for short videos including TED Talks that are publicly available and can assist me.
I am working on Conversational Competence in a business setting and am looking for articles that give me tips for how to improve.

Key Soft Skill: Confidence

Exercise: Daily Affirmations
Write and repeat three positive statements about yourself each day to boost self-belief. Tape them to your bathroom mirror. Do this four weeks in a row.

Exercise: Move That Body
Physical activity can improve mood and self-esteem, making you feel more confident. Make a table of physical activity you will do each day of the week. Tape it to your bedroom door. Choose activities that take less than ten minutes. For example, walking, push-ups, climbing stairs, jumping jacks. Do this four weeks in a row.

Exercise: Looking Good
Wear clothes that make you feel good about yourself, as this can positively impact your confidence. Assemble five outfits that you look great in. Wear them five days in a row. Repeat for three more weeks.

AI Companion prompts:
I am working on Confidence in a business setting and am looking for short videos including TED Talks that are publicly available and can assist me.
I am working on Confidence in a business setting and am looking for articles that have tips for how to improve.

Key Soft Skill: Positivity

Exercise: Make Them Laugh
Purposely call a service person on the phone (order pizza, ask an insurance question, schedule appointment) and try to get them to laugh.

Exercise: Smile Tour
Work on eye contact and smiling. Smile and get someone to smile back. See how many smiles you can collect during a walk or errand.

Exercise: Daily Joke
Call or text a friend (or group of friends) with a light-hearted joke or funny stories each day. Tip: collect a few on Sunday to use throughout the week.

AI Companion prompts:
I am working on Positivity in a business setting and am looking for short videos including TED Talks that are publicly available and can assist me.
I am working on Positivity in a business setting and am looking for articles that have tips for how to improve.

Key Soft Skill: Charisma

Exercise: Present Moment Pause
Take a few moments each day to focus entirely on the present moment and the person you're with, avoiding distractions like your phone.

Exercise: Storytime Spark
Share a personal story with someone each day, focusing on making it interesting and relatable.

Exercise: Enthusiasm Express
Before noon each day, express excitement about something, whether it's a project at work or a personal hobby with someone in your path.

AI Companion prompts:
I am working on Charisma in a business setting and am looking for short videos including TED Talks that are publicly available and can assist me.
I am working on Charisma in a business setting and am looking for articles that have tips for how to improve.

—THE BE-SOCIAL METHOD —

GET TO KNOW MORE PEOPLE • SELF-ASSESSMENT

Building Blocks:

What are your joys?

What are you working on?

Who do you know but are not caught up with, but would like to be?

Who have you met that you would like to get to know?

Get to Know More People Practices:

#1 – Exchange "elevator speeches" and stories.

- How often do you do this practice?
  Circle answer: Always, Sometimes, Never

- What activities do you currently do that would give you the opportunity to work on this practice?

_____

_____

_____

- How could you tie working on this practice to one of your joys?

_____

_____

_____

#2 – Join an organization (professional, charitable, hobby/special interest, religious, political) and lead a group such as a committee.

- How often do you do this practice?
  Circle answer: Always, Sometimes, Never

- What activities do you currently do that would give you the opportunity to work on this practice?

_____

_____

_____

- How could you tie working on this practice to one of your joys?

#3 - Invite someone to network over coffee/video call—less than thirty minutes.

- How often do you do this practice?
  Circle answer: Always, Sometimes, Never
- What activities do you currently do that would give you the opportunity to work on this practice?

- How could you tie working on this practice to one of your joys?

#4 - Invite someone to network over lunch/drinks/dinner—one hour plus.

- How often do you do this practice?
  Circle answer: Always, Sometimes, Never

- What activities do you currently do that would give you the opportunity to work on this practice?

- How could you tie working on this practice to one of your joys?

#5 - Engage digitally with someone to get to know them via extended chat or text.

- How often do you do this practice?
  Circle answer: Always, Sometimes, Never
- What activities do you currently do that would give you the opportunity to work on this practice?

- How could you tie working on this practice to one of your joys?

HOW TO PUT THIS INTO ACTION

Review the following five *Get to Know More People Practices*. Decide which practice you will focus on. The practice you pick can be one that you think is easier than the others or a practice that you want to push yourself to try. Tell a trusted friend your plan and make it happen!

Get to Know More People Practices (pick one to focus on):

- ☐ Exchange elevator speeches and stories.

- ☐ Join an organization (professional, charitable, hobby/special interest, religious, political) and lead a group such as a committee.

- ☐ Invite someone to network over coffee/video call—less than thirty minutes.

- ☐ Invite someone to network over lunch/drinks/dinner—one hour plus.

- ☐ Engage digitally with someone to get to know them via extended chat or text.

Discuss with your team member the following points:

- In business, we are always looking to strengthen relationships with one another. The better we know people, the more likely we will think of each other for new opportunities and respond to requests for help.

- In our personal lives, we can and should work on these practices while doing things we are already doing and enjoy.

- Bonus: Doing the *Get to Know More People Practices* regularly results in the strengthening of these key soft skills:

  - Initiative
  - Prioritization
  - Planning and Organization
  - Curiosity

Ask your team member to review their *Get to Know More People Self-Assessment* responses.

Afterward, ask your team member if the set of practices seems EASY or HARD to them.

- If your team member answers EASY, look at the practices assessed as *Sometimes* or *Never*. Discuss which of these practices the can work on doing *Always*.
  - Note here ideas for doing the practices at work.

_____

_____

  - Note here at least one way the team member will do the practices through their joys.

_____

_____

- If your team member answers HARD, look over the list of related key soft skills.
  - Check which of these skills they need to work on.
    - ☐ Initiative
    - ☐ Prioritization
    - ☐ Planning and Organization
    - ☐ Curiosity
- Provide them the *Get to Know More People Exercises and Resources* and discuss. Note here at least one of the exercises they plan to try or resources they plan to reference.

_____

_____

The Be-Social Method
Get to Know More People

Exercises and Resources

Key Soft Skill: Initiative

☐ **Exercise: My Project**
Choose a small, manageable project that interests you and commit to completing it within one month. This could be anything from organizing a community event to starting a blog. Tell five people you are working on it and expect to have it done by the end of the month.

☐ **Exercise: Three Daily Goals**
Pick a friend to text your three daily goals to each day by noon. Do this for four weeks. Make sure the goals can be done in one day. Track the number of days you text your goals by noon.

☐ **Exercise: That Bugs Me**
Identify a small problem or inefficiency in your daily routine or environment. Take one proactive step each day to address it and share your progress with a friend weekly. Track your steps for four weeks.

☐ **Book:**
Initiative: A Proven Method to Bring Your Passions to Life (and Work)
by Joshua Spodek

☐ **AI Companion prompts:**
I am working on Initiative in a business setting and am looking for short videos including TED Talks that are publicly available and can assist me.
I am working on Initiative in a business setting and am looking for articles that give me tips for how to improve.

Key Soft Skill: Prioritization

☐ **Exercise: Daily Ranking**
Each morning, list all tasks you need to complete for the day. Rank them in order of importance and tackle them accordingly. Keep track of how many days you do the ranking over four weeks.

☐
Exercise: Eisenhower Matrix
Use the Eisenhower Matrix to categorize your daily tasks into four quadrants: urgent and important, important but not urgent, urgent but not important, and neither. Focus on the important tasks first. Do this for four weeks.

☐
Exercise: Not Today
Identify and eliminate or delegate at least one nonessential task from your to-do list each day. Track the number of days you successfully eliminate or delegate a task over a four-week period.

☐
AI Companion prompts:
I am working on Prioritization in a business setting and am looking for short videos including TED Talks that are publicly available and can assist me.
I am working on Prioritization in a business setting and am looking for articles that have tips for how to improve.

Key Soft Skill: Planning and Organization

☐
Exercise: Break it Down
Take a large project you plan to accomplish within two to four weeks and list all the steps it will take to complete it. Put the steps in the order you need to do them and give each step a target date for completion. Once a week, update your list by removing completed steps and adjusting target dates.

☐
Exercise: Daily To-Do List
Each morning, write a to-do list of tasks you need to complete for the day. Prioritize them and check off each task as you complete it. Track the number of days you complete your to-do list over four weeks.

☐
Exercise: Time Blocking
Allocate specific time blocks for different tasks or activities throughout your day. Write the schedule down. Stick to the schedule as closely as possible. Track the number of days you adhere to your time blocks over four weeks.

AI Companion prompts:
I am working on Planning and Organization in a business setting and am looking for short videos including TED Talks that are publicly available and can assist me.
I am working on Planning and Organization in a business setting and am looking for articles that have tips for how to improve.

Key Soft Skill: Curiosity

Exercise: Daily Question
Each day, write down one question about something you're curious about. Spend at least fifteen minutes researching the answer. Track the number of days you write down one question you're curious about over four weeks and how many of those days you spend fifteen minutes researching the answer.

Exercise: Tell Me More About That
Each day ask someone you encounter what they did over the weekend. Ask them to tell you more about one of the activities they mentioned. Say in a pleasant way, "Tell me more about that." Track the number of "Tell me more" conversations you have over a four-week period.

Exercise: Expert in the House
Each day ask someone you encounter, "What do you do for fun?" Ask them questions to learn more about their interest. Track the number of experts you identify over a four-week period.

AI Companion prompts:
I am working on Curiosity in a business setting and am looking for short videos including TED Talks that are publicly available and can assist me.
I am working on Curiosity in a business setting and am looking for articles that have tips for how to improve.

THE BE-SOCIAL METHOD

CONNECT PEOPLE • SELF-ASSESSMENT

Building Blocks:

What are your joys?

_____

_____

_____

What are you working on?

_____

_____

_____

Who in your network would be good to introduce to each other?

_____

_____

_____

Who in your network would be good to reconnect (They know each other but are not caught up)?

_____

_____

_____

Connect People Practices:

#1 – Introduce people to each other at events/meetings.

- How often do you do this practice?
  Circle answer: Always, Sometimes, Never

- What activities do you currently do that would give you the opportunity to work on this practice?

- How could you tie working on this practice to one of your joys?

#2 – Introduce people to each other over email or text (five-minute favor).

- How often do you do this practice?
  Circle answer: Always, Sometimes, Never

- What activities do you currently do that would give you the opportunity to work on this practice?

- How could you tie working on this practice to one of your joys?

#3 – Spend time considering who you connect and why. (Be selective.)

- How often do you do this practice?
  Circle answer: Always, Sometimes, Never

- What activities do you currently do that would give you the opportunity to work on this practice?

- How could you tie working on this practice to one of your joys?

#4 – Introduce a small group (two to three others) to each other at an event hosted by you.

- How often do you do this practice?
  Circle answer: Always, Sometimes, Never

- What activities do you currently do that would give you the opportunity to work on this practice?

_____

_____

_____

- How could you tie working on this practice to one of your joys?

_____

_____

#5 - Host a large (four people or more) event for people to meet or reconnect with others.

- How often do you do this practice?
  Circle answer: Always, Sometimes, Never

- What activities do you currently do that would give you the opportunity to work on this practice?

_____

_____

_____

- How could you tie working on this practice to one of your joys?

HOW TO PUT THIS INTO ACTION

Review the following five *Connect People Practices*. Decide which practice you will focus on. The practice you pick can be one that you think is easier than the others or a practice that you want to push yourself to try. Tell a trusted friend your plan and make it happen!

Connect People Practices (pick one to focus on):

☐ Introduce people to each other at events/meetings.

☐ Introduce people to each other over email or text (five-minute favor).

☐ Spend time considering who you connect and why.

☐ Introduce a small group (two or three others) to each other at an event hosted by you.

☐ Host a large (four people or more) event for people to meet or reconnect with others.

Discuss with your team member the following points:

- Mastering the *Connect People* practices is essential.

- In business, we are always looking to create new opportunities and solve problems.

- Being able to rapidly connect people and get them working collaboratively on solutions is a basic skill of the best leaders.

- In our personal lives, we can, and should, work on these practices while doing things we are already doing and enjoy.

- Bonus: Doing the *Connect People Practices* regularly results in the strengthening of these key soft skills:

  - Empathy
  - Facilitation
  - Event planning
  - Creativity

Ask your team member to review their *Connect People Self-Assessment* responses.

Afterward, ask your team member if the set of practices seems EASY or HARD to them.

- If your team member answers EASY, look at the practices assessed as *Sometimes* or *Never*. Discuss which of these practices the can work on doing *Always*.

  - Note here ideas for doing the practices at work.

  - Note here at least one way the team member will do the practices through their joys.

- If your team member answers HARD, look over the list of related key soft skills.
- Check which of these skills they feel weak in.
  - ☐ Empathy
  - ☐ Facilitation
  - ☐ Event planning
  - ☐ Creativity
- Provide them the *Connect People Exercises and Resources* and discuss. Note here at least one of the exercises they plan to try or resources they plan to reference.

The Be-Social Method
Connect People
Exercises and Resources

Key Soft Skill: Empathy

Exercise: Send Twelve Angels
Identify up to twelve people you know who are struggling with something specific. Take time each day to visualize them and their struggle. Send them support through your positive thoughts. Visualize that you have twelve angels who can go and sit by the people on your list. Then assign each angel to go out to each person on your list. (You can send more than one angel to each person.) Do this for four weeks.

Exercise: Encourage Youth
Have a ten-minute conversation with a child, teen, or young adult. Ask and share your answers to these questions: What do you do for fun? What are you working on? (Smile, make eye contact, listen actively, be enthusiastic, provide no unsolicited advice.) Do this once a week for four weeks.

Exercise: Favorite Photos
Ask someone about a photo in their home or office. Ask them to describe the photo to you. Then ask them why they chose to save that particular photo. Seek to understand the story behind the photo. Do this once a week for four weeks.

Book:
How to Have Impossible Conversations: A Very Practical Guide by Peter Boghossian and James Lindsay

AI Companion prompts:
I am working on Empathy in a business setting and am looking for short videos including TED Talks that are publicly available and can assist me.
I am working on Empathy in a business setting and am looking for articles that give me tips for how to improve.

Key Soft Skill: Facilitation

Exercise: Break the Ice
Before leaving your home for an outing whether it's to go to work, the grocery store, church, the gym, or a party, come up with two questions you can ask someone you encounter. Have one of the questions be situational and one be about current events in your community. Do this daily for four weeks.

Exercise: Feedback Collector
Facilitate a feedback session with a friend or family member on a recent event they hosted. Ask what went well, what could have gone better, and what recommendations they have for future events. Summarize it and send it to the organizer. Be careful to hold back your personal feedback.

Exercise: Purpose Protector
Enter social situations with a clear sense of purpose. For example, ask yourself what the primary purpose of your social event is. Is it to affirm your affection or connection, catch up, or offer support to a specific problem? Monitor your behavior accordingly and steer others appropriately.

AI Companion prompts:
I am working on Facilitation in a business setting and am looking for short videos including TED Talks that are publicly available and can assist me.
I am working on Facilitation in a business setting and am looking for articles that have tips for how to improve.

Key Soft Skill: Event Planning

Exercise: Your Event
Brainstorm an event you would like to host. Tie it to one of your joys, whether that's a baseball game, a concert, or a backyard barbecue. Decide the number of guests you would like to attend, when it would begin and end, the tasks needed to get it organized, the budget you need, and adjust as needed. Run the design by a trusted friend and adjust further as needed.

Exercise: Be My Guest
Brainstorm a guest list for an event you would like to host within the next year. Adjust the list as you consider the right mix of people to invite to your event and the number you think will likely decline due to other obligations. Also consider how early you would need to send out the invitations to increase the likelihood invitees will be able to attend. Determine how you will track RSVPs. Run the list and RSVP tracking method by a trusted friend and adjust as needed.

Exercise: Plan to Join Me
Create a promotion plan for an event you would like to host within the next year. Brainstorm ways that you could let your invitees know about your event in advance of the formal invitation and ways you could keep them excited about the event after the invitation has been sent to get more to respond yes and fewer to cancel at the last minute. Run your promotion plan by a trusted friend and adjust as needed.

Book:
The Art of Gathering: How We Meet and Why It Matters by Priya Parker

AI Companion prompts:
I am working on Event Planning in a business setting and am looking for short videos including TED Talks that are publicly available and can assist me.
I am working on Event Planning in a business setting and am looking for articles that have tips for how to improve.

Key Soft Skill: Creativity

Exercise: Walk and Wonder
Take a daily walk in a new environment, such as a park, neighborhood, or museum. Observe your surroundings and note anything that sparks your creativity, or use your phone to take a picture of it and refer to it later.

Exercise: Creative Reading
Read a book, article, or story outside your usual genre or field of interest. Reflect on how the new perspectives can inspire your own creative projects.

Exercise: My Creative Time
Set a daily creative challenge for yourself, such as drawing a picture, writing a poem, or designing a logo. Complete the challenge within a set time limit, for example thirty minutes or one hour. Consider selecting a place and time of day where you will consistently do your creative work. Target doing this every day for four weeks. Keep track.

AI Companion prompts:
I am working on Creativity in a business setting and am looking for short videos including TED Talks that are publicly available and can assist me.
I am working on Creativity in a business setting and am looking for articles that have tips for how to improve.

—THE BE-SOCIAL METHOD —

Building Blocks:

What are your joys?

What are you working on?

What do you need help with?

Who could help you?

Ask for Help Practices:

#1 – Set a goal and strategy for achieving it that includes leveraging your network.

- How often do you do this practice?
  Circle answer: Always, Sometimes, Never

- What activities do you currently do that would give you the opportunity to work on this practice?

- How could you tie working on this practice to one of your joys?

#2 – Clearly articulate what you need help with.

- How often do you do this practice?
  Circle answer: Always, Sometimes, Never

- What activities do you currently do that would give you the opportunity to work on this practice?

- How could you tie working on this practice to one of your joys?

#3 – Ask for help from someone you know and are current with.

- How often do you do this practice?
  Circle answer: Always, Sometimes, Never
- What activities do you currently do that would give you the opportunity to work on this practice?

- How could you tie working on this practice to one of your joys?

#4 – Reach out to someone you know but are not current with to ask for help.

- How often do you do this practice?
  Circle answer: Always, Sometimes, Never

- What activities do you currently do that would give you the opportunity to work on this practice?

- How could you tie working on this practice to one of your joys?

#5 - Ask someone you don't know for help.

- How often do you do this practice?
  Circle answer: Always, Sometimes, Never
- What activities do you currently do that would give you the opportunity to work on this practice?

- How could you tie working on this practice to one of your joys?

HOW TO PUT THIS INTO ACTION

Review the five *Ask for Help Practices*. Decide which practice you will focus on. It can be one that you think is easier than the others or one that you want to push yourself to try.

Ask for Help Practices (pick one to focus on):

- ☐ Set a goal and strategy for achieving it that includes leveraging your network.
- ☐ Clearly articulate what you need help with.
- ☐ Ask someone you know and are caught up with for help.
- ☐ Reach out to someone you know but are not caught up with for help.
- ☐ Ask someone you don't know at all for help (such as an expert or someone you admire).

Discuss with your team member the following points:

- Mastering the *Ask for Help* practices is essential.

- In business, a team that works together gets a better outcome. Working together requires asking others for help and depending on that help.

- In our personal lives, we can, and should, work on these practices while doing things we are already doing and enjoy.

- Bonus: Doing the *Ask for Help Practices* regularly results in the strengthening of these key soft skills:
  - Vulnerability (courage)
  - Humility (strength)
  - Trust
  - Care (self and others)

Ask your team member to review their *Ask for Help Self-Assessment* responses.

Afterward, ask your team member if the set of practices seems EASY or HARD to them.

- If your team member answers EASY, look over with them the items they selected *Sometimes* or *Never*. Discuss which of these practices they can work on doing *Always*.

- Note here ideas for doing the practices at work.

- Note here at least one way the team member will do the practices through their joys.

- If your team member answers HARD, look over the list of related key soft skills.
  - Check which of these skills they feel weak in.
    - ☐ Vulnerability (courage)
    - ☐ Humility (strength)
    - ☐ Trust
    - ☐ Care (self and others)
- Provide them the *Ask for Help Exercises and Resources* and discuss. Note here at least one of the exercises they plan to try or resources they plan to reference.

The Be-Social Method
Ask for Help
Exercises and Resources

Key Soft Skill: Vulnerability (courage)

Exercise: Eye Contact Practice
Practice maintaining eye contact with people during conversations. Start with short durations and gradually increase the time.

Exercise: Learn from Others
Pick something you want to learn about. Consider who could help you learn about it. Reach out with a specific learning request. Have the ask be "bite-sized."

Exercise: I Have a Question
Pick a live event to attend where there will be a question-and-answer session. Prepare some questions in advance. Attend the session (bring an accountability partner) and ask at least one question.

Book:
Rejection Proof: How I Beat Fear and Became Invincible Through 100 Days of Rejection
by Jia Jiang

Book:
Super Mentors: The Ordinary Person's Guide to Asking Extraordinary People for Help
by Eric Koester and Adam Saven

AI Companion prompts:
I am working on Vulnerability (courage) in a business setting and am looking for short videos including TED Talks that are publicly available and can assist me.
I am working on Vulnerability (courage) in a business setting and am looking for articles that give me tips for how to improve.

Key Soft Skill: Humility (strength)

Exercise: Admit Mistakes
Reflect on your day and identify any mistakes you made. Write them down and/or acknowledge them openly with a friend or family member and discuss what you learned.

Exercise: Feedback is a Gift
Ask for feedback from a friend on an approach you are taking to solve a problem that you think is rock solid. Resist the temptation to defend your approach. Instead seek to understand their constructive criticism. Thank them for their feedback and consider how you can use it to improve.

Exercise: Gratitude Sharing
Each day, acknowledge your dependence on others in your life by sharing your appreciation for the support they give you with a friend or family member.

AI Companion prompts:
I am working on Humility (strength) in a business setting and am looking for short videos including TED Talks that are publicly available and can assist me.
I am working on Humility (strength) in a business setting and am looking for articles that have tips for how to improve.

Key Soft Skill: Trust

Exercise: Task Complete
Select someone to demonstrate your ability to complete a task or promise each day. Then each day, tell them the task you will do for them. Then follow through on this task by completing it that day. Do this for four weeks. Track your success rate.

Exercise: The Real Me. The Real You.
Catch up with someone. Share with them what you are working on personally and professionally. Share your successes and setbacks. Encourage them to do the same.

Exercise: Check In, Even if it Feels Awkward
Demonstrate to someone that you care about them and their success by checking in with them on a particular struggle they shared with you. Don't worry about how much time has passed.

Book:
Move Fast & Fix Things: The Trusted Leader's Guide to Solving Hard Problems
by Frances Frei and Anne Morriss

AI Companion prompts:
I am working on Trust in a business setting and am looking for short videos including TED Talks that are publicly available and can assist me.
I am working on Trust in a business setting and am looking for articles that have tips for how to improve.

Key Soft Skill: Care (self and others)

Exercise: Daily Self-Care Routine
Dedicate at least fifteen minutes each day to a self-care activity, such as meditation, reading, or taking a walk. Focus on activities that help you relax and recharge. Do this for four weeks. Track your progress.

Exercise: Help Around the House
Ask someone you live with to do a chore for you every day for four weeks. Break it down so it becomes something that can be accomplished within thirty minutes. The shorter the better. If they grumble, ignore it. If they do not do it as well as you would have, ignore this. Focus instead on their completing the task. Thank them.

Exercise: Healthy Habits
Incorporate a healthy habit into your daily routine, such as drinking more water, eating nutritious meals, or getting enough sleep. Focus on a habit that will improve your overall well-being. Track your progress over four weeks.

Book:
Showing Up: A Comprehensive Guide to Comfort and Connection by Jen Marr with Skye Quinn

Book:
The Art of Asking or How I Learned to Stop Worrying and Let People Help by Amanda Palmer

AI Companion prompts:
I am working on Care (self and others) in a business setting and am looking for short videos including TED Talks that are publicly available and can assist me.
I am working on Care (self and others) in a business setting and am looking for articles that have tips for how to improve.

NOTES

INTRODUCTION

Paul Fireman. "The Truth about Teens, Social Media and the Mental Health Crisis." Children's Health Council. 2024. https://www.chconline.org/resourcelibrary/the-truth-about-teens-social-media-and-the-mental-health-crisis/.

CIGNA. "Loneliness and Its Impact on the American Workplace: Understanding the Drivers of Workplace Loneliness, the Costs and the Solutions." 2024. https://legacy.cigna.com/static/www-cigna-com/docs/about-us/newsroom/studies-and-reports/combatting-loneliness/loneliness-and-its-impact-on-the-american-workplace.pdf.

Jenny Fernandez, Kathryn Landis, and Julie Lee. "Helping Gen Z Employees Find Their Place at Work." *Harvard Business Review*. January 18, 2023. https://hbr.org/2023/01/helping-gen-z-employees-find-their-place-at-work.

Mitchell Hartman. "The Cost of Loneliness: Social Isolation Holds Back Workers and Costs Employers

Billions." *Marketplace*. March 1, 2023. https://www. marketplace.org/2023/03/01/the-cost-of-loneliness-social-isolation-holds-back-workers-and-costs-employers-billions/.

Kathleen Schulz. "Employee Wellbeing—The Human & Economic Cost of Loneliness: How Work-From-Home Mandates Affect Loneliness and Social Isolation." *Gallagher US*. https://www.ajg.com/us/news-and-insights/2020/aug/employee-wellbeing-human-economic-cost-loneliness/.

Rick Hecht. "How Employee Loneliness Impacts the Workplace." *CuraLinc Healthcare*. February 9, 2023. https://curalinc.com/blog/loneliness.

3 in 4 Managers Find It Difficult to Work with GenZ." 2024. ResumeBuilder.Com. March 22. https://www.resumebuilder.com/3-in-4-managers-find-it-difficult-to-work-with-genz/

Katherine Bindley and Chip Cutter. "Young People Are Taking Over the Workplace, and That's a Problem for Bosses." *The Wall Street Journal*, September 2, 2024. https://www.wsj.com/lifestyle/careers/gen-z-workforce-expectation-differences-a07c5915?mod=hp_trending_now_article_pos1.

Jane Thier. "Managers' Latest Complaints about Gen Z: They Lack Soft Skills and Have Unrealistic Workplace Expectations." *Yahoo! Finance*. January 23, 2024. https://finance.yahoo.com/news/managers-latest-complaints-gen-z-173000484.html.

Huileng Tan. "3 in 4 Managers Say Gen Z Is the Most Challenging Generation to Work with and 40% of the Group Flagged a Lack of Technological Skills, Effort, and Motivation: Survey." *Business Insider*. April 20, 2023. https://www.businessinsider.com/gen-z-managers-employees-most-challenging-technological-skills-survey-2023-4.

Resume Builder. "3 in 4 Managers Find It Difficult to Work with GenZ." *ResumeBuilder.com*. April 17, 2023. https://www.resumebuilder.com/3-in-4-managers-find-it-difficult-to-work-with-genz/.

Taylor Penley. "Why Gen Z Surpassing Boomers at Work Is Troubling for Managers: 'Age of Authority Is Dropping.'" *FOX News*, September 2024. https://www.msn.com/en-ca/money/career/why-gen-z-surpassing-boomers-at-work-is-troubling-for-managers-age-of-authority-is-dropping/ar-AA1q6JiV?ocid=BingNewsSerp.

Suzanne Blake. "Gen Z Has a Loneliness Problem." *Newsweek*. March 7, 2024. https://www.newsweek.com/generation-genz-loneliness-problem-mental-health-1877013.

Erica Pandey. "The Loneliest Generation: Inside the Gen Z Mental Health Crisis." *AXIOS*, February 17, 2024. https://www.axios.com/2024/02/17/gen-z-depression-anxiety-future-workforce.

Bret Austin. "Gen Z + Mental Health: What Is Impacting Our Youth and Young Adults Today?" *UofL Health*. Louisville Hospital and Health Care System. May 8, 2023. https://uoflhealth.org/articles/gen-z-mental-health-what-is-impacting-our-youth-and-young-adults-today/.

Caryl M. Stern. "A Slow-Motion Crisis: Gen Z's Battle Against Depression, Addiction, Hopelessness." *The 74*. September 7, 2022. https://www.the74million.org/article/a-slow-motion-crisis-gen-zs-battle-against-depression-addiction-hopelessness/.

Mitchell Hartman. "The Cost of Loneliness," cited earlier.

Kathleen Schulz. "Employee Wellbeing—The Human & Economic Cost of Loneliness," cited earlier.

Rick Hecht. "How Employee Loneliness Impacts the Workplace," cited earlier.

Elizabeth Bondy and Dorene D. Ross. "The Teacher as Warm Demander." *ASCD*. September 1, 2008. https://ascd.org/el/articles/the-teacher-as-warm-demander.

Matt Alexander. "The Warm Demander: An Equity Approach." *Edutopia*. George Lucas Educational Foundation. April 13, 2016. https://www.edutopia.org/blog/warm-demander-equity-approach-matt-alexander.

Jessica Wei Huang. "4 Practices of Warm Demander Teachers." *Edutopia*. George Lucas Educational Foundation. November 28, 2023. https://www.edutopia.org/article/4-practices-warm-demander-educators.

Cogent Analytics. "Introduction to SCARF Model in Change Management." *Cogent Analytics*. https://www.cogentanalytics.com/knowledge-center/introduction-to-scarf-model-in-change-management/.

Deloitte. "Understanding Generation Z in the Workplace: New Employee Engagement Tactics for Changing

Demographics." *Deloitte United States*. https://www2.deloitte.com/us/en/pages/consumer-business/articles/understanding-generation-z-in-the-workplace.html.

Dean Guida. "Gen Z Is Using Data to Drive Performance. Here's How to Get the Rest of Your Company to Do the Same." *Entrepreneur*. December 7, 2023. https://www.entrepreneur.com/leadership/gen-z-is-using-data-to-drive-performance-heres-how-to-do/462344.

PART I

While some research points to Gen X as being best suited to address Gen Z's needs for leaders who can address their need for trusted leaders who inspire them, I believe leaders of any generation can be warm demander leaders.

Expert Panel. "15 Ways Leaders Can More Effectively Manage Gen-Z Workers." *Forbes.* January 17, 2023. https://www.forbes.com/councils/forbescoachescouncil/2023/01/17/15-ways-leaders-can-effectively-manage-gen-z-workers/.

Chapter 1

Orianna Rosa Royle. "Gen Z Has No Idea How to Interact with Their Coworkers—and It Could Cost Them a Promotion." *Fortune.* January 23, 2024. https://fortune.com/2024/01/23/gen-z-social-skills-limited-coworkers-promotion/.

John Hall. "How to Help Gen Z Early-Career Professionals Navigate Careers." *Harvard Business Publishing.* May 15, 2024. https://www.harvardbusiness.org/how-to-help-gen-z-early-career-professionals-navigate-their-careers/.

Ana Homayoun. "The Invisible Handbook of Skills Gen Z Employees Lack." *Fast Company.* July 21, 2023. https://www.fastcompany.com/90925354/the-invisible-handbook-of-skills-gen-z-employees-lack.

Peter Gray. *Free to Learn: Why Unleashing the Instinct to Play Will Make Our Children Happier, More Self-Reliant, and Better Students for Life.* Basic Books, 2013.

Consultancy Services Team. "11 Top Tips for Managing Gen Z Employees." *FDM Group.* July 6, 2024. https://www.fdmgroup.com/news-insights/managing-gen-z-employees/.

CIGNA. "Are You Feeling Lonely?" Cigna Healthcare Newsroom. https://newsroom.cigna.com/loneliness-questionnaire.

Judith Kleinfeld. "Effective Teachers of Eskimo and Indian Students." *The School Review*, 83, February 1975.

Kathy Neesen. "Students, Especially African-Americans, Thrive with Warm, Demanding Teachers." *UVA Today*. March 8, 2017. https://news.virginia.edu/content/students-especially-african-americans-thrive-warm-demanding-teachers.

Carrie Furrer and Ellen Skinner. "Sense of Relatedness as a Factor in Children's Academic Engagement and Performance." *Journal of Educational Psychology*, 95 (1).

Lia E. Sandilos, Sara E. Rimm-Kaufman, and Julia J. Cohen. "Warmth and Demand: The Relation Between Students' Perceptions of the Classroom Environment and Achievement Growth." *Child Development*, 88 (4), 2017.

Jenny Fernandez et al. "Helping Gen Z Employees Find Their Place at Work," cited earlier.

Milton Campbell. "What Motivates Gen Z in the Workplace: 8 Simple Ways." *Growth Tactics*. December 22, 2023. https://www.growthtactics.net/what-motivates-gen-z-in-the-workplace/.

Adam Smiley Poswolsky. "Gen Z Employees Are Feeling Disconnected. Here's How Employers Can Help." *Harvard Business Review*. June 13, 2022. https://hbr.org/2022/06/gen-z-employees-are-feeling-disconnected-heres-how-employers-can-help.

Karolina Wennqvist. "What Motivates Gen Z Employees at Work? Insights into How Leaders Can Create a Workplace Environment Where the Motivational Needs of Gen Z Are Met." Master's thesis, International Business Management. 2022.

PART II

Bianca Alves. "Gen Z in the Workplace: Statistics and 2024 Trends." JOB TODAY. 2024. https://jobtoday.com/us/blog/gen-z-in-the-workplace-statistics-and-2024-trends/.

Resume Builder. "3 in 4 Managers Find It Difficult to Work with GenZ," cited earlier.

Jack Flynn. "25+ Gen Z Statistics [2023]: Tech, Preferences, and More." Zippia. May 9, 2023. https://www.zippia.com/advice/gen-z-statistics/.

Chapter 8

Catherine Clifford. "Billionaire CEO Jamie Dimon: 7 Simple Rules to Follow to Be a Successful Boss." CNBC make it. April 11, 2019. https://www.cnbc.com/2019/04/11/jpmorgan-chase-ceo-jamie-dimon-rules-to-be-a-successful-boss.html.

Paige McGlauflin. "JPMorgan CEO Jamie Dimon Chides Managers Who Work from Home." *Fortune*, July 11, 2023. https://fortune.com/2023/07/11/jpmorgan-ceo-jamie-dimon-scolds-managers-work-from-home-accessible-leader/?utm_source=search&utm_medium=suggested_search&utm_campaign=search_link_clicks

"Introversion." *Psychology Today*. https://www.psychologytoday.com/us/basics/introversion.

"Extroversion." Psychology Today. https://www.psychologytoday.com/us/basics/extroversion.

Jennifer Guttman. "Introvert vs. Extrovert: How Does It Affect Social Anxiety?" Cognitive Behavior Therapy. February 15, 2021. https://www.guttmanpsychology.com/2021/02/15/introvert-vs-extrovert-how-does-it-affect-social-anxiety/.

Chapter 9

Corporate English Solutions. "Gen Z in the Workplace: Bridging the Soft Skills Gap to Drive Success." British Council. February 12, 2024. https://corporate.britishcouncil.org/insights/gen-z-workplace-bridging-soft-skills-gap-drive-success.

María Dolores Benítez-Márquez, Eva María Sánchez-Teba, Guillermo Bermúdez-González, and Emma Sofía Núñez-Rydman. "Generation Z Within the Workforce and in the Workplace: A Bibliometric Analysis." *Frontiers in Psychology* 12, January 31, 1011.

"4 in 10 Business Leaders Say Recent College Grads Are Unprepared to Enter Workforce." Intelligent. August 30, 2023. https://www.intelligent.com/4-in-10-business-leaders-say-recent-college-grads-are-unprepared-to-enter-workforce/.

Bruce Tulgan. "What Is the Soft Skills Gap." Training Industry. January 22, 2018. https://trainingindustry.com/blog/leadership/what-is-the-soft-skills-gap/.

Colleen McFarland. "Hardening Needed." Medium. May 1, 2024. https://medium.com/realness-meaning-and-belonging-at-work/hardening-needed-6e07de16eeae.

Jean M. Twenge. *iGen: Why Today's Super-Connected Kids Are Growing Up Less Rebellious, More Tolerant, Less Happy—and Completely Unprepared for Adulthood (and What This Means for the Rest of Us.* Atria Books, 2018.

Jean M. Twenge. "Meet iGen: The New Generation of Workers That Is Almost Everything Millennials Aren't." Quartz. January 11, 2018. https://qz.com/work/1177712/igen-the-new-young-generation-of-workers-is-almost-everything-that-millennials-are-not.

Amy Porterfield. "The Simplest Step By Step Process." Digital Course Academy. https://www.amyporterfield.com/digitalcourseacademy-3?rootabl=a997&msclkid=877e88110d2714fb2e3feeffc5806405.

"2023 Work in America Survey: Workplaces as Engines of Psychological Health and Well-Being." American Psychological

Association. 2024. https://www.apa.org/pubs/reports/
work-in-america/2023-workplace-health-well-being.

PART III

"LIVE: Shaka Smart Introduced as New Marquette Basketball
Coach: LIVE: Officials Are Introducing Shaka Smart, 43,
as the New Head Coach of Marquette University's Men's
Basketball Team." WISN 12 NEWS. Facebook.

https://www.facebook.com/watch/
live/?ref=watch_permalink&v=159418099374429.

"Shaka Smart: Marquette Men's Basketball Postgame Press
Conference." YouTube. February 7, 2023. https://www.
youtube.com/watch?v=4s_YPdaiipw.

How You Can Help

Megan Carnegie. "Are Gen Z the Most Stressed Generation
in the Workplace?" BBC News. February 16, 2023. https://
www.bbc.com/worklife/article/20230215-are-gen-z-the-most-
stressed-generation-in-the-workplace.

Andrea Yu. "Why Gen Z Workers Are Already So Burned
Out." BBC News. May 26, 2022. https://www.bbc.com/
worklife/article/20220520-why-gen-z-workers-are-already-so-
burned-out.

Madeline Garfinkle. "They Think They're Better Than You:
74% of Managers Surveyed Say Gen Z Is More Difficult to

Work with Than Other Generations." Entrepreneur. April 20, 2023. https://www.entrepreneur.com/business-news/managers-on-gen-z-difficult-at-work-and-lack-discipline/450064.

Karina Ochis. "Five Steps Toward Improving Gen-Z Employee Performance: A Primer for Managers." Forbes. May 4, 2023. https://www.forbes.com/councils/forbes-coachescouncil/2023/05/04/five-steps-toward-improving-gen-z-employee-performance-a-primer-for-managers/.

Suzanne Blake. "Gen Z Has a Loneliness Problem," cited earlier.

Bret Austin. "Gen Z + Mental Health: What Is Impacting Our Youth and Young Adults Today?" cited earlier.

Caryl M. Stern. "A Slow-Motion Crisis: Gen Z's Battle," cited earlier.

ABOUT THE AUTHOR

Colleen McFarland knows what it takes to motivate individuals to do the hard work that change requires. She has decades of experience helping executives lead their people through workplace changes. She coaches leaders to bring out the full potential of employees by adopting a warm demander leadership style.

Colleen's passion is business networking. She is the creator of "How Wrigley Field Made Me a Better Networker," a workshop that features the Be-Social Method, that she has delivered since 2016.

Her first book, *Disconnected*, published in April 2020 explores how technology has not only changed how we work, but us, too, especially Gen Z.

She is the proud and grateful mother of two sons, Daniel and Christopher McFarland, who are Gen Zers and always willing to share their point of view with her.

She and her husband, John McFarland, split their time between Dunedin, Florida and Chicago, Illinois.

Colleen hopes you join her in addressing the mental health crisis facing young adults by being a model and promoter of relationship building in the workplace and in your personal life.